LAW OF
SUCCESSION

LAW OF SUCCESSION

IAN JONES, LLB (Hons) (Wales), Solicitor
Senior Lecturer in Law, Manchester Metropolitan University

Series Editor C. J. CARR, MA, BCL

BLACKSTONE
PRESS LIMITED

First published in Great Britain 1993 by Blackstone Press Limited, 9-15 Aldine Street, London W12 8AW. Telephone: 081-740 1173

ISBN: 1 85431 199 9

British Library Cataloguing in Publication Data
A CIP catalogue record for this book is available from the British Library

Typeset by Montage Studios Limited, Tonbridge, Kent
Printed by BPCC Wheatons Ltd, Exeter

Cartoons drawn by Paul Muirhead

CONTENTS

TO
SATHA
&
PM

PREFACE

This is not a textbook. The purpose of this book is to provide an aid and revision guide to the study of succession, i.e., transmission of property on death. The law of succession, however, is well served by first class textbooks and books on cases and materials, so why should you buy this book? I believe that it will assist in revision for examinations, whether leading to academic or professional qualifications, and I hope that it will stimulate the study of this important subject. I have derived enjoyment over the years from talks to all types of students, i.e., from full-time or part-time students, to those pursuing correspondence courses both in this country and overseas. I hope that you will enjoy studying this subject, for enjoyment fuels interest which leads to success.

This book would not have been possible without the inspiration and support given by the team at Blackstone Press. They have given their advice in a professional and friendly way which has served to help the author.

To mention individual students who represent the real success over the years would be lengthy, and it would also be unfair to those who are left out. The inspiration provided by those students, however, and the bond formed, is summed up in the dedication.

INTRODUCTION

Will England win the soccer World Cup again? It came close in 1990 but in the view of Brightman J in *Moore* v *Griffiths* [1972] 3 All ER 399 its chances appear slim. He commented that he could not see any forseeable recurrence of the bonus payment to the 1966 winning squad. However, the purpose of this book is not to speculate upon the future success of soccer teams, but to look to your success in the study of the law of succession.

Succession is the branch of property law which deals with the transmission of property on the death of an individual. The subject builds upon knowledge acquired from prior studies, in particular in relation to equity and trust law, and is complementary to studies in taxation. The subject remains a popular academic study, as well as forming an integral part of the framework of professional examinations for intending solicitors and legal executives.

Law studies take many forms. As you read this book you may be already embarked upon full-time studies. Alternatively, you may be studying part-time or soldiering on, without the contact of fellow students, by means of self-study, with or without the aid of a correspondence course. This book has been written as a support to your studies whatever form they take. It is not a textbook, but it aims to provide another angle to your study of the standard textbooks and the source material by putting together various points in a way intended to stimulate and inform. Study can be a lonely business. Even where you attend full-time classes, with fellow students around you, at the end of the day it is up to you, the individual, how you convey the acquired knowledge to the assessor through the examination and assessed work.

Law studies can provide a trap even for the most conscientious of students. The cornerstones of law studies are the primary source material, statutory provisions and the decisions of the courts. A great deal of time can be wasted if the student does not know the way through the source material. By the time the undergraduate, or student studying for professional examinations, reaches the law of succession it is to be hoped that study techniques will have been fine tuned to analyse quickly the case, or to see the significance of a particular statutory provision. Alas, this is not always borne out in answers to examination questions. Perhaps the mind has wandered in the course of studies to the speculation concerning a possible England success, or indeed for whichever team you support. The initial aim of this work is to keep the studies on track. The aims and methods of study, and points on examination technique are considered in chapters 1 and 2, before comentary upon the law of testate and intestate succession in the remaining chapters of the book.

ONE

STUDY TECHNIQUES

Introduction

The purpose of this chapter is to explain the thinking and mechanics which lie behind the delivery of a course of study in order that you may relate the points to your particular studies.

The principal aim of law studies for the vast majority of students is success in examinations leading to work within the legal profession. Approximately eighty per cent of graduates with first degrees in law enter professional practice, the majority as solicitors with most of the remainder at the Bar. In addition, an increasingly popular route in recent years has been for non-law graduates to enter the profession by taking the Common Professional Examination. Further, there have been important developments in the career grades for membership of the Institute of Legal Executives; now Fellowship of the Institute can lead on to entry for the final examinations to qualify as a solicitor.

In the main the comments upon study techniques in this work are made from the viewpoint of studies in a first degree in law. However, they are relevant for the candidate facing professional examinations for entry into the legal profession.

Law studies, be they first degree or the first stages of professional examinations, are built around a core of study of key subjects, for example, the distinction between civil and criminal law; the contrasting civil obligations of contract and tort; the legal system itself, how it is formed, how it works; rights and obligations in the law of property. The study of succession builds upon these initial key studies in property law. Succession is offered as an option in the final year studies on law degree courses, either as a subject in its own right, or as part of a course on the transmission of property, or as part of studies in taxation. Indeed, in legal practice, the form of the will is an integral part of many tax planning schemes.

The aim of study

Course structures are founded upon the basis that students will acquire skills and competence in all the areas of the received conventional taxonomy. These areas can be summarised as follows.

(a)   Knowledge — of the appropriate terminology, e.g., testator, executor, probate, administration; specific facts and the major concepts and principles.
(b)   Comprehension — recognition, selection and interpretation of relevant information presented in varying forms; understanding how to collect and process information.
(c)   Application — using appropriate terminology and applying appropriate concepts to explain complex issues.
(d)   Analysis — to distinguish reason from assertion, and fact from value.
(e)   Synthesis — recognition and application of inter-related elements which together promote understanding of complex issues.
(f)   Evaluation — the ability to recognise the reliability of information so as to form reasoned judgment.
(g)   Expression — to present and communicate information, analysis, evaluations and conclusions with clarity, accuracy and in an appropriate form.

Consider carefully the progression through this list, from the acquisition of knowledge, through application and analysis, to expression, given not only the importance of the most common form of evaluation, i.e., the three hour unseen examination, but the increasing movement towards assignment-driven modules. There is a strong movement towards studies being not simply acquisition of facts and a demonstration of comprehension, but with greater emphasis being placed upon analysis and evaluation. There is a continuing movement in first degree studies towards student centred learning. In studies for professional examinations there is increasing emphasis being placed upon communication skills, and less upon the acquisition and storage or a mass of factual information, although in law studies it is inevitable that the student acquires a great deal of factual knowledge and, indeed, part of the skill of the practitioner is to grasp and retain facts quickly. However, the real skill lies in being able to analyse situations; to identify grey areas or areas of doubt in statutory provisions; or to cut through a long report of a key judgment.

Where to begin

Those embarking on a study of succession will, in the majority of cases, be familiar with the most common method of course delivery, i.e., the attendance at lectures, backed by a series of seminars and/or tutorials. The terms tutorial and seminar tend to be inter-changeable in many institutions, albeit the seminar tends to denote a group discussion of say ten upwards, whereas tutorials tend to be groups of five or six. In some centres of learning the tutorial remains a one-to-one experience between the tutor and pupil. In many institutions if the student is in a one-to-one situation this usually means the other four have failed to turn up!

The lecture

The purpose of the lecture should be to provide a way of viewing a particular topic by making available a key for unlocking the multitude of points which arise from a particular area of study. The lecture should stimulate, amuse, and above all command attention. The method of delivery will vary according to the number of students in attendance. In the case of the core subject areas of study in a major centre of higher education the numbers attending can be well over one hundred. This kind of volume does not encourage questions, for, in responding to a particular question, the lecturer cannot always command the attention of all students and time is lost in the consequential distraction. This does not mean that the lecture should be some long monotonous delivery of facts with the students, heads down, scribbling away. Students should be stimulated into turning to the texts and, more importantly, the major sources of the law, statute and case reports.

In the case of the smaller group, more likely in second or third year options, the lecturer will have more scope to create a dialogue. This can stimulate so long as it does not distract by the lecturer losing the thread of the main points of the topic of the day. The added danger in a question and answer approach is the encouragement of the individual student who wishes to show off acquired knowledge. A well founded point made by an individual student can be encouraging for it can show that someone is understanding, but the frequency of interruptions from particular individuals can cause dismay to the remainder of the audience. The lecturer, as the guide, must strike the balance between encouragement, and progress through the syllabus. The student, as the recipient, must learn to strike the balance between listening to what is said (this is harder and less obvious than it reads) and taking a note sufficient to provide an *aide memoire* to further study.

Supplementary and supportive material

Modern technology enables the rapid production of a whole range of handout material. This can be both useful and dangerous. When the aim is to supplement, the deliverer must ask 'where do I draw the line?'. The danger is in giving too much material, to 'cover' the subject. In order to deal with as many points as possible the lecturer is faced with giving increasing quantities of additional material by way of handout. Ideally the learning process should be selective and the lecturer, as the guide, should concentrate upon the key issues.

In the case of supportive material, the handout can either take the form of a framework for the lecture, where the lecturer then proceeds to fill in the gaps, or the handout is a summary *per se* of the lecture. There is a danger in the first method for both the lecturer and the students may treat the lecture as a 'painting by numbers' exercise, simply spending the time filling in the blanks, the students not listening, and the lecturer not necessarily presenting a clear, coherent argument. In the second case, i.e., where the handout is a summary, if the handout is given at the start of the lecture, there is a temptation not to listen and, following the 'video' mentality, the student files the handout believing that he or she has read it!

On balance, if a handout is to be used, it should provide a framework of the key points of the lecture. This has the advantage of avoiding a student's natural tendency to write everything down, and should encourage the student to listen to the lecturer. The framework method ensures that the student has the key headings, assuming the student reads through the lecture material soon after the lecture. Sadly, some full time students believe that simply turning up to the lecture will enable some kind of absorption of knowledge by osmosis to occur, leaving them free to rent a video of more general entertainment. The moment of truth often arrives too late when they wish the lecturer, or at best a friend, is sitting in their place in the examination room!

The good lecture should provide the launch pad to self-study, by building up the understanding of a topic or study in preparation for discussion of a particular statement or problem in a tutorial.

The tutorial

The tutorial is used to aid comprehension and to enable the student to apply and analyse the knowledge by tackling a problem. The ability to analyse and evaluate a problem lies at the heart of law studies. Sound preparation for the tutorial is essential. Poor preparation is not simply a personal let down; it is disappointing for the tutor and fails to contribute to lively debate which is the hall mark of the tutorial of value. When studies reach the stage of second and third year options, or the final part of professional examinations, such as in the case of succession, it is assumed that the basic skills of preparation have been mastered. The tutorial problem should, in conjunction with the lecture, encourage the student to go to the sources. So often, however, there is simply a cursory reading of the textbook and no more. There is a disappointing tendency for students to leap into the middle of a problem giving a brief explanation of one issue which they have recognised. The sound approach is to consider the problem line by line, assemble the key points and research the authorities so that clear points can be made in a discussion, backed by authority.

Where the tutorial topic is not complementary to a lecture, then the researching of the problem starts with reading the relevant text and making a note of key points and sources. Do not make notes from the text on a first reading, for this approach can lead you into taking too detailed a note, virtually writing the text verbatim. Re-read the text and then make notes of the key points and sources. The tutorial information itself may take the form of a 'paper-chase' in which you are led through a series of primary sources. Even here, read through the text first and then go to the primary sources.

The approach to the sources

The primary source material comprises statutory provisions and the case authorities.

Statute

In a tutorial problem attention could be drawn to a particular section or sub-section. In problems on intestacy a favourite topic is the entitlement of the surviving spouse to the personal chattels as defined by s. 55(1)(x) of the Administration of Estates Act 1925. A sound approach would be to read the relevant part of the text first, then the wording of paragraph (x) noting the list of particular items followed by the general words '. . . articles of personal use and enjoyment . . .', and then note the case authorities to research later. There may be additional material available which provides commentary upon the section, either giving the reasons for the statutory provision or comments upon possible reform. In the case of paragraph (x), for example, there is commentary upon reform in the Law Commission Report, No. 187 (1989). An example of the reasons for a particular statutory provision is the background to s. 1 of the Wills Act 1968 which arose following the Court of Appeal decision in *Re Bravda* [1968] 2 All ER 217.

In analysing a tutorial problem, it is possible that attention will have been directed to a particular section or sub-section. In law studies in general there are key statutory provisions which stand out in particular topics. In the tutorial, possibly in the examination, you would have the statutory provisions to hand. Even so, this is no substitute for knowing certain key sections thoroughly. The example of sub-paragraph (x) has been given as a popular topic. In the study of succession a line by line knowledge of the formal requirements for the making and revocation of wills is essential. To understand fully the requirements as to form in s. 9 of the Wills Act 1837 the original statutory provisions need to be studied, followed by the reasoning behind and wording of the section as amended by s. 17 of the Administration of Justice Act 1982. The 1982 Act followed the Law Reform Report No. 22 'The making and breaking of wills'. A detailed knowledge of ss. 17-21 of the 1982 Act is essential.

Case authorities

The life blood of the law is to be found in the cases. However clear a text may be, and in the study of succession there are excellent texts, there is no substitute for reading the cases. This does not simply mean the headnote and then back to the pool table! When a case is read carefully the facts tend to stick in the mind, and this aids later revision. The subject becomes more stimulating as the arguments unravel. Study the arguments of counsel and see if you agree with the judge. Consider what leeway, if any, the court had in considering the application of a particular statutory provision. A good example is the attitude of the courts to s. 15 of the Wills Act 1837 which denies a benefit to a witness beneficiary. See how, through the cases, the courts have tried to narrow the application of the section, and examine the lack of room to manoeuvre in *Re Bravda* (1968).

When you can demonstrate to the tutor that you have read the cases then everyone is stimulated. Reading is one thing of course, understanding is another. Don't be afraid to return to the text for guidance in seeking to understand the arguments in a long report. Start with basic points and then work up. Where you are enrolled upon full- or part-time study, do not simply say 'oh, I'll ask her in the tutorial', hoping that the tutor will launch into a monologue, but demonstrate that you have read the judgments and then ask the questions. You will receive a much warmer response if you demonstrate that you have made an effort yourself.

Reading the reports is not easy. There is a great risk in law studies that even the most industrious, conscientious student can thrash about in the undergrowth failing to see the path to clear issues and the significance of the particular case. Study is not easy. Sound study comes with practice. Unfortunately many students think that acquiring sound study techniques, and the consequential acquisition of knowledge, occurs through a process not unlike cross-pollination whereby knowledge is scattered like dust. This type of student usually seeks the 'dust' not as one might think in the library, but in the learned hostelry, forgetting that worthwhile debate is founded upon the acquisition of skills. Too often students forget that their studies are part of a building process. They tend to compartmentalise, and once a stage of examinations is finished they forget all about legal process, or tort or contract or whatever. They cannot put away fast enough the agonising over e.g., *ratio*, *obiter*, *per incuriam*, as if they were a series of high graded ski-runs. They do not appreciate that those earlier subjects were providing the base for sound case analysis. Remember that the headnote is merely what it says it is, it is not the complete story, merely a window, and not always a clear window at that. A first instance decision will contain the presentation of the facts and the arguments on both sides. In an appeal case you need to consider whether it is a unanimous decision or split. If it is split, you should find out whether there is a strong dissenting judgment. For example, read Lord Denning in *Re Rowland* [1962] 2 All ER 837. Where the split is in the House of Lords then you are presented with a major review. An example of this is the key decision on the interpretation of s. 184 of the Law of Property Act 1925, i.e., *Hickman* v *Peacey* [1945] AC 304. There are other 'gems' apart from the arguments on both sides; for example, the extracts from the lengthy will of the redoubtable Lord St. Leonards in *Sugden* v *Lord St. Leonards* (1876) 1 PD 154; the overview of mental capacity by Cockburn CJ in *Banks* v *Goodfellow* (1870) LR 5 QB 549 or the review and interpretation of 'actual military service' by Arnold P in *Re Jones* [1976] 1 All ER 593.

Learn to pick out the leading decisions upon a topic and through these analyse the problem. The tutorial problem itself will usually be constructed to highlight the difficulty or uncertainty within a given topic. Remember that there is not necessarily a hard and fast solution. The purpose is for you to construct and elucidate the arguments through your understanding of the authorities.

The assignment

More and more courses are introducing assessments and moving away from the idea that the final grade should depend upon the performance in a series of three hour unseen examinations. An increasing number of individual subjects determine their end of year mark by 20 to 25 per cent or more by assessment, and the remainder by examination. In some cases the grade in an entire subject can depend upon a series of assignments or one dissertation. The importance of the assessed work cannot be understated. The onus is clearly on the student to achieve a high grade. In the previous section the importance of a well prepared approach to the tutorial was stressed. In tackling an assessment the groundwork, so important in sound tutorial performance, is all the more important.

Consider carefully what is required. The assessment may consist of a case study followed by a series of questions; a problem with the request to advise X or simply a proposition which you are asked to consider, comment on, or criticise. Refer again to the aims of study set out at the beginning of this chapter. An assessed work will be seeking not only to test comprehension but will require a demonstration of analytical skills, synthesis, evaluation and clear expression.

Note the conditions of the assessment, in particular format, length and how this is calculated and the submission date. Bear in mind that both length and submission dates require strict adherence.

There can be problems with regard to assignments both for the conscientious student and the lackadaisical one. However enthusiastic the student may be at the start of a long assignment, boredom and loss of interest can set in. Groundwork should be done when you are fired by enthusiasm and writing up should not be left long after the groundwork notes have been completed, otherwise the notes have to be read and re-read in order to set the drive in motion to write the work in a flowing, coherent manner. The great danger in the case of the idle candidate is the reluctance to start. There is always some excuse which prevents the person putting pen to paper. The result is that everything is left to the last minute; groundwork is sketchy and the final submission is perfunctory. The majority of the marks will be devoted to the substantive content. Does the work display a succinctly expressed understanding of the issues, analysis of identified problems and an evaluation backed by a sound conclusion? Do not, however, detract from considerable effort, together with time spent in the library, by poor presentation. The conditions of submission may specify a typed script. In a long work there is a danger of underestimating the time taken in turning the draft into a presentable form. Always allow adequate time for presentation so that there is still time to deal with unexpected delays.

The value of the assignment is in presenting the student with the opportunity to submit work which achieves a high grade thereby reducing the dependence upon the examination. In addition the assignment teaches self-discipline, the ability to organise material and, hopefully, the ability to write in a concise, coherent way. Where the form of the assignment is a longer work, a project or major dissertation, a good grade can be a useful pointer to future work and references. However, do not forget that assignments only make up a part of the grading and in legal education great store is still set by the performance in the examinations. Therefore, in planning time to devote to assignments, do not let other work, particularly preparation for tutorials, suffer. Approach the assignment in a positive way to gain enjoyment from the effort. A worthwhile piece of work will give pleasure and satisfaction but seek also to strike a balance with other work.

Reading

Try to be more diligent than one student who, when a textbook was mentioned and the tutor asked (with a hint of despair in his voice) 'have you read it or are you going to read it?' replied 'are there any pictures?'.

The study of the law of succession is blessed with excellent texts. The leading textbook is *Parry and Clark's The Law of Succession*, 9th ed. (Sweet & Maxwell, 1988). The textbook does not have pictures (!) but is comprehensive and authoritative. The text includes the revised Non-Contentious Probate Rules 1987 in full as an appendix; example clauses in will drafting and the order of application of assets in the insolvent estate revised by the Insolvency Act 1986. In addition a number of important cases have been included since the previous edition in 1983.

The other leading textbook was *Mellows's The Law of Succession*, 4th ed. (Butterworths, 1983). Unfortunately there has not been an edition since 1983 and the book can no longer be recommended in view of its age. This is a pity for Professor Mellows writes with authority and humour.

Butterworths publishes a very good volume of *Cases and Materials on Succession* by Cherry Wright. The book cover has a reproduction of a painting entitled 'A Flaw in the Will' by Philip Richard Morris 1836-1902, but this is not the reason for purchase! The book is extremely useful as an adjunct to *Parry and Clark*, containing extracts from cases and reports. Study of the book will equip the student with a wider dimension of the subject.

Parry and Clark and the casebook by Wright are both recommended for purchase. In considering further reading, you should turn to the practitioners' books such as *Theobald on Wills* and the recently revised *Williams on Wills*. In addition to numerous case references these large volumes contain many individual clauses and specimen wills. *Tyler's Family Provision*, 2nd ed., by R. D. Oughton provides a comprehensive practitioners' guide to this important topic.

Although the law of succession does not experience frequent change, or have the multiplicity of more recent cases as, for example, tort or criminal law, the subject is dynamic. In addition to litigation the law is reviewed and study should be made of the Law Reform Committee's 22nd report, 'The Making and Revocation of Wills' (1980) Cmnd 7902. The report contains a wide ranging review. The conclusions led directly (albeit with a time lag for parliamentary time for the legislation) to the important revisions in the law made by the Administration of Justice Act 1982.

More recently the Law Commission Report on Intestate Distribution, No. 187 (1989) contains a review of the present law on intestacy. In addition a survey was undertaken of will making among different age groups and social backgrounds. The Law Commission has prepared draft legislation. Whether the government will take up the suggestions and, if so, when, is another matter. The Morton Committee Report in 1950 (Cmnd 8310) led to a re-casting of intestate distribution by the Intestate Estates Act 1952. Time will tell whether the major changes proposed by the Law Commission in the 1989 report will become law.

Probate law comprises an important part of private client work for the practising solicitor. Journals such as the *Law Society's Gazette* and the *New Law Journal* provide articles, recent case summaries and changes in practice. For example, two very good articles on family provision appeared in the *Law Society's Gazette* in 1986. In the first article, R. D. Oughton considered the issue of provision for the adult child following the decision of the Court of Appeal in *Re Leach* [1985] 3 WLR 413 and the second article was by J. G. Ross-Martyn on precautions and possible pitfalls in the legislation.

The indexes of the *Modern Law Review*, *Law Quarterly Review* and the *Conveyancer* reveal useful, in-depth articles. In addition a search through journals from further afield can result in interesting and thought-provoking material which can give a wider dimension to issues. A good example is the article by John H. Langbein, 'The Non-Probate Revolution and the Future of the Law of Succession' which appeared in issue number 97 of the *Harvard Law Review*.

Family Law, in addition to case reports, particularly but not exclusively on family provision, contains articles; for example, an article by C. H. Sherrin on the making of a statutory will for a patient pursuant to s. 96 of the Mental Health Act 1983, appeared in (1983) 13 *Family Law* 135.

The primary sources, legislation and the cases should be studied carefully. Recent case law can prompt examination questions and a thorough knowledge of the key statutory provisions will provide a sound base.

Legislation

The starting point must be the Wills Act 1837. The key sections will stand out in the course of study. The Wills Act must be coupled with the important changes effected by the Administration of Justice Act 1982. Additional legislation includes the Intestates' Estates Act 1952; the Family Law Reform Acts of 1969 and 1987; the Inheritance (Provision for Family and Dependants) Act 1975; the Forfeiture Act 1982; the Wills Act 1968 and the Insolvency Act 1986.

There are important sectional references to the Administration of Estates Act 1925, the Trustee Act 1925 and the Supreme Court Act 1981. In addition study should be made of the Non-Contentious Probate Rules 1987, in particular the order for priority in obtaining a grant of letters of administration contained in rules 20 and 22.

Certain sections should be known thoroughly, for example, s. 46 of the Administration of Estates Act 1925 for the priority of interests on intestacy; s. 34(3) of, and part II of sch. 1 to the Administration of Estates Act 1925 for the order of payment of debts in an insolvent estate; and the Insolvency Act

1986 coupled with the Administration of Estates of Deceased Persons Order SI 1986 No. 1999 for the order of payment of debts in an insolvent estate.

The Administration of Justice Act 1982, in particular ss. 17 to 21, made a number of important changes to the law of succession. Section 17, for example, sets out the revised s. 9 of the Wills Act 1837. This should be known line by line since formal validity is crucial to the completion of the will-making process, and an obvious area for examination questions.

A good exercise is to set out separately each section of the 1982 Act: s. 17 (the revised s. 9 of the Wills Act 1837); s. 18 (revocation by marriage and the exceptions); s. 18A (the effect of divorce or annulment); s. 19 (the revised s. 33 of the Wills Act 1837); s. 20 (rectification) and s. 21 (construction and the admission of the extrinsic evidence). These changes are so important that they constantly form key points in examination questions.

In applying a knowledge of legislation in answering questions do not adopt a tunnel vision. Try and consider the interpretation as a whole. A study of reports enables the student to adopt a broader brush approach in setting a topic in context. So often in answering problem questions the student has plunged head down into detailed parts. Has there been a valid acknowledgement? Is Lucy debarred from benefiting because she is a witness? Is the car left by the intestate deceased a personal chattel?

Higher marks can be obtained in some situations by making reference to wider considerations stemming from background often provided by the debate of issues in a particular report. For example, one could be asked to consider the proposition that the definition of personal chattels in s. 55(1)(x) of the Administration of Estates Act 1925 is outmoded. The Law Commission has recommended that the surviving spouse should receive the whole of the estate on an intestacy. This would obviate the need for a consideration of individual chattels in an intestacy question, although many wills bequeath personal chattels by reference to s. 55(1)(x). Why is the section considered to be outmoded? In tackling this question one should not give a list of various examples of the interpretation of the section through the cases. Adopt a wider view. Look for example, at the structure of the section, i.e., the general reference to articles of personal use and enjoyment coupled with the particular list of articles with a rather dated air.

Another example is the approach to s. 184 of the Law of Property Act 1925 which deals with commorientes. Consider carefully what the section says and how it has been interpreted. The leading case is *Hickman* v *Peacey* [1945] AC 304. The case turned upon the meaning of the word 'uncertain'. Therefore, in explaining the section, do not use loose language but use the precise word 'uncertain'. In addition, read carefully the exception to the application of the statutory presumption in the case of spouses where the older or both die intestate and ask why there should be a need for this exception.

Do not fall into the trap of thinking that a good answer to a problem is simply reeling off a series of section references or sub-sections in an attempt to impress the examiner with your memory. A good example of this trap is in answering problem questions on family provision. Certainly it is important to know who has *locus standi* to apply, as set out in s. 1(1)(a) to (e) of the Inheritance (Provision for Family and Dependants) Act 1975. However to convey an understanding of the Act it is important to explain how these sub-paragraphs have been interpreted by reference to the cases. For example, you will need to be able to explain what is meant by 'child of the family' or 'dependant'. It is no good simply saying 'Alice can claim by virtue of s. 1(1)(d)' or 'Emily can claim as a result of s. (1)(e)'. Cite the dicta in *Re Leach* (1985) on the meaning of 'child of the family'. Consider how the courts weigh contributions in dependency as explained in *Jelley* v *Iliffe* [1981] 2 All ER 29, CA, with further commentary by the Court of Appeal in *Bishop* v *Plumley* [1991] 1 All ER 236. This does not mean just a passing reference but a demonstration from your commentary that you have read the judgments of Slade LJ in *Re Leach* (1985), Stephenson LJ in *Jelley* v *Iliffe* (1981) and Butler-Sloss LJ in *Bishop* v *Plumley* (1991). Sound technique is not demonstrating some form of memory test of numerous sections, but conveying an understanding of the issues. The key is how the statutory provisions have been interpreted by the courts.

The important topic of the capacity to make a will provides a good example of the need to study the common law as there is no statutory definition of the mental capacity required to form the *animus testandi*. However, this does not mean scattering numerous cases with little commentary throughout your answer, but demonstrating an understanding of the issues and approach as illustrated through the judgments.

Studying reports and articles enables the student to appreciate commentary and provide the broader view. For example, consider the proposition that the Administration of Justice Act 1982 only made minor changes to the law of succession when a thorough modernisation of the law was required. Consideration of this proposition does not mean listing in detail the requirements of the revised s. 9 of the Wills Act 1837. Certainly include an explanation of the changes regarding the positioning of the signature of the testator — and this still does not mean anywhere on the will (!) — and the ability of the witnesses to acknowledge their signatures. However, take a broader view. The Law Reform Committee report of 1974 referred to striking a balance between protection from fraud (the former s. 9) and avoiding mere 'mechanical' failure. In *Re Colling* (1972) there was no suggestion of fraud or improper motive, the timing of the events simply fell foul of s. 9. Should our system adopt a less formal approach? Refer to the Langbein articles, Langbein, John H., 'The Non-probate revolution and the future of the Law of Succession', 97 *Harvard Law Review* 1108, which pointed out the range of private property which passes with the minimum of formality (for example, pension rights and entitlement under policies of life assurance). The proposition is not confined to the revised s. 9. One could consider the power to rectify in s. 20. Has this gone far enough? Does s. 21 represent a codification of the law on the admission of extrinsic evidence? Where does the balance lie between protection against fraud and an easing of the requirements on formal validity? Should our system adopt the doctrine of substantial compliance? Should the courts have greater flexibility to correct errors, or is this treading the path of writing the will for the testator? Study of commentaries and reports can enable the student to adopt a wider view and more critical approach.

TWO

REVISION AND EXAMINATION TECHNIQUES

The purpose

For many students success in the examination is the ultimate goal. It is why this book is being read! Time will show that the end is merely the beginning, but for the time being let us concentrate on that date at the end of the course, the examination. The unseen, time-constrained examination remains the main form of assessment in law studies — why? Because study for examinations concentrates the mind, teaches the student to sort out the main material from the peripheral and gives the chance to demonstrate the ability to comprehend, analyse quickly and communicate in a succinct way. Remember it is the quality of the script and not the width which matters!

Revision

The building of the base for sound revision really starts from the commencement of the studies of the subject. Law studies are not simply a collection of facts. Although an essential part of the study is assimilation of factual information, this information cannot be carried by simply reading and re-reading the textbook. A set of notes needs to be built up. The material should consist of notes made in lectures, with or without handout material, notes from a reading of the text and support material together with notes taken of studies of the primary source material. Spend time putting this material in some order and ensure that collectively it makes sense. Do not re-write lecture notes, this is a waste of time. You can disagree with this, but really it is a waste of time. Far more is gained by additional reading of the source material. Do not simply file lecture notes away so that they next see the light of day a few weeks (if you are thinking in terms of a few days you have got problems) before the examinations.

Some courses have a high volume of handout material in addition to your own notes. Invest in decent files to keep the material in order. Do not be a bag man. How often have you seen the person who carries all the notes on the option, or even more than one option, in one jumbled mass in a large bag with last week's sports pages, two ball point pens and a half eaten packet of mints? This individual will spend more time trying to make sense out of the material and looking for missing sheets, than he will spend in the library.

Revision therefore should start from a sound base. You will be surprised how much has been retained in the memory where sound preparation has been the benchmark through the year. The judgment read is the judgment retained. Revision should not consist of darting from a note to a frantic flipping of the pages of the textbook to clarify a point, followed by the telephone call to the friend with 'have you got a copy of the lecture on anti-avoidance in family provision?'. The material should have been collated so that, although points may occur which you check by reference to the text or a report, there are no 'grey areas' where information which should have been there has disappeared into a void of earlier sloth.

So, the material is in order. What method should be adopted? No writer, however well intentioned, can be prescriptive about how you go about your revision. Should you read through an entire topic once? Should you read and re-read the material? Should you read and make notes condensing the topic? Whichever method you choose, you must choose the one which suits you as an individual. Be careful, however, if you are one of those who likes to write summaries of your material. Do not do this until you have read it so that you are familiar with it, otherwise you run the risk of simply writing out your notes again virtually in full, which is a waste of time.

Organise your time so that preparation is not left until the eleventh hour. Time management is vital, not only in allotting time to the different subjects but in ensuring that energy is maintained. Do not lose sleep, it is simply not worth it. This is not to say that you should casually go off fishing the night before the examination, because being keyed up concentrates the mind, but if you enter the examination room tired out even the most obvious points will escape you, as you sit there thinking 'how many witnesses need there be for a will?' or, even worse, 'what is a will?'.

The day itself

Make sure you get the right day. This may seem ridiculous but it does happen and the following conversation, or one like it, occurs each year. 'Oh, this isn't the day for contract then?' 'No.'

Relax. You have done all you could. Relaxation helps concentration. Go to your appointed seat. Make sure, where a large examination room is accommodating several courses, that you have the right desk. Do not (it has been known) stand there shouting 'I can't do it, I can't do it', until a friend, looking over your shoulder, points out that that desk is for the maths candidate and that you are here to display your knowledge of succession.

The paper

You have purchased this book for a purpose. The book is not there to prop
up the table so that the television is not on a slant. The book is to read and to
assist you in your studies. So, the cardinal rule is to read — read the
examination paper. It is not there to be made into paper aeroplanes, it is
there to be read carefully, not going slowly over 'Monday 6 June' — you
know what day it is — but read the rubric. This is not a cube but refers to the
number of questions you are asked to attempt. Look particularly for
questions expressed in an either/or form. So many candidates continue to
answer both parts. If you are allowed, make notes against the different
questions on your first reading. The points may take longer to recall when
you are busy writing the answers. Read every question carefully before you
decide which ones you are going to answer.

Questions in a problem form

In seminar and tutorial work prior to the examination you will have to
prepare answers to questions set in a problem form. Indeed it is likely that
through the course, and certainly in the examination, the majority of the
questions will be in a problem form. Ask yourself 'what are the main issues
here?' If you find yourself asking, 'why is this sentence in?', you are more
than likely missing a point which the examiner wants you to pursue. Make
sure you identify in your mind all the key points and understand all the
factual references: if you do not, do not answer the question. The facts
themselves will prompt you to pick out the relevant cases from your revision.

Do not 'scan read' the question looking for a general reference to a topic
which you have revised. This is dangerous, your answer will lack relevance
and you can make incorrect assumptions. It is surprising, for example, how
often, in problem questions involving two people, Henry and Wendy, that
the candidate, in a cursory reading, assumes that the parties are married
when the question does not say so. 'Scan reading', i.e., looking vainly to
recognise a topic from a limited revision, can result in the 'write all I know'
syndrome. For example, there is a problem question involving a mistress
and a possible child of the family where the candidate is asked to advise upon
an application under the Inheritance Act 1975. Many answers start by listing
all those who have *locus standi* under the 1975 Act. This is irrelevant, for the
question concerns only two possible categories. This fault can be evidence of
the 'thank goodness' syndrome — 'thank goodness, there is something on
family provision; I can write all I know'. Family provision is a topic which has
a great influence in the law of succession. Given the wider categories of
potential claimant under the 1975 Act, considerations of fairness to
dependants and close family members can come into virtually any question

involving beneficial distribution under a will or intestacy. This is why it is important to read the actual question at the end of the problem to see what is required. The question will either make it clear whether or not aspects of family provision are to be considered, or the question could specifically exclude reference to the 1975 Act.

How should you approach the problem question? Consider the issues as revealed by the facts of the question. Do not drag other issues in, stay relevant and within the confines of the question. Identify the key issues, e.g., 'this question is concerned with the ability to form a clear *animus testandi*'. Develop the answer by explaining the issue, e.g., 'in order to have the capacity to make a valid will the testator must have sound mind, memory and understanding'. Back your development of the law with authority. For example, a reference to the judgment of Cockburn CJ in *Banks* v *Goodfellow* (1870) LR 5 QB 549 and an explanation of what is meant by sound mind, memory and understanding (see chapter 3), bringing in additional case authorities and illustrations, will be needed.

Where the question asks you to advise Henry as to, for example, the admissibility of the will to probate, make sure in your conclusion that you advise Henry. Remember, there will, more than likely, be no clear cut answer. The purpose of the question is to assess whether you comprehend the issues, can analyse the problem and articulate the answer by providing arguments both ways. Don't just write 'sue him' and turn to another question, this is a perilous course which can lead to rather a low mark.

The question is often asked — 'what should I remember about a case?'. The key points are the ratio, an important dissenting dictum, the facts of the case and the arguments followed by the name. However, a failure to cite the name accurately of a leading case can be an indication of poor preparation. A statement such as 'this is a case on the meaning of the word "money" — *Pegleg* v *Morton* . . .' is bad news. Just as bad is 'there was this case'. The problem is there to see whether you can recognise the problem, argue, back your argument with authority whilst adopting a clear, concise style.

The essay

Sound essay technique is important not only in your contribution through the course and performance in the examination but in developing the skill of delivery of a clearly argued opinion.

The essay should be both clearly expressed and concise. Careful consideration should be given to the question. This might appear to be obvious but it is surprising how many students read what they want to see and not necessarily what the question actually says. For example, does the question ask you to critically consider a particular issue? If so, an answer which is largely descriptive will gain little, if any, credit.

In setting the essay topic the tutor is looking for your views and your understanding of the issues. The essay should have a definable form: a short introduction outlining your ideas; the points you wish to make, supported by authorities; and a short conclusion.

Where the essay is part of the seminar programme or as part of a continuous assessment, you should receive some indication of the expected length. In an examination you will be facing a time constraint. The long essay is of course no guarantee of a high grade. Little credit is given for long descriptive pieces which may include numerous quotes. The tutor will be looking for a demonstration of your understanding of the topic and your views on a particular proposition or critique. A key purpose of the essay is to develop your skills in communication. Sound preparation is the key. A careful study should be made on the sources with some note-taking followed by a draft framework. The essay should then be written in your own words. Certainly cite authorities, sources and where appropriate, use quotes. However, remember the tutor is assessing your ability to comprehend the material and convey the comprehension in a clear, concise way. Lengthy quotes should be avoided as they can interrupt the flow.

Sometimes students treat written work set during the course as an opportunity to write all they know about a particular topic instead of confining their answer to the question. This is done with the intention of using this material as an aid to revision for the examination. This approach is a mistake as it ignores the purpose behind the setting of the written work, namely, to test comprehension of the particular issue and the ability to marshall the arguments in a clear, concise manner. Where the essay forms part of the formal assessment leading to a final grade on the course the need for relevance and a strict adherence to the question asked and the instructions given is vital.

Verbal presentation   During the series of seminars a tutor may request that a student gives a verbal presentation to the tutor and fellow students. This does not simply mean reading the essay verbatim. You are being asked to present a case and your arguments in answer to the proposition. To ensure a clear presentation you need to be thoroughly prepared.

In some courses the use of visual aids is offered, such as overhead projectors or write to screen television projectors. Where you are going to use equipment of this nature, prepare sheets containing key headings. Where equipment is not being used but you are requested to make a presentation before an audience a useful aid is to write key headings on cards. These can act as a prompt and aid your delivery by pacing your presentation. A thorough knowledge of your topic coupled with the ability to respond to questions is the sign of the well prepared presentor. There is a growing emphasis upon the ability to make a sound verbal presentation as part of the increasing emphasis upon skills in legal education. Sound preparation and a clear exposition is a great boost to individual confidence.

Let us return to the hurdle of the examination. Where you decide to answer an essay question, read the question carefully. Consider what is being asked and whether you can effectively deal with all the issues. Draft a framework as part of your rough work and calculate the maximum time you can allow yourself for the answer. Make sure you stick to your framework.

Timing

Timing is crucial. Does your examination paper ask you to answer four, five or more questions? Is there a compulsory question which carries more marks? Is the paper divided into parts with the requirement to answer a minimum number of questions from each part? Once you have chosen the questions to be attempted, work out the time you need to allot to each answer and stick to it. Remember, if you have to answer four questions on a three hour paper, with each question carrying equal marks, you are marked out of 25 per question. It is easier to score the first six to eight marks than it is to score the last ten. Therefore it is extremely foolish to miscalculate your time so that there is little left to start the fourth question. You are penalising yourself out of stupidity.

Style

Try to write clearly. Avoid note form even where you are rushed towards the end. Many courses and centres use answer books which saves a multiplicity of sheets of paper. If you do have extra papers make sure that each one is clearly identified and that they are securely fastened together.

Conclusion

Many of these points come easily to the well prepared person who has taken a clear headed but relaxed attitude. Each individual has their own routine in settling to start the examination. This is fine, so long as you do not disturb your neighbour and do not cover the desk with so many lucky souvenirs that you cannot find the examination paper!

The material on technique is to make you reflect and adopt a relaxed, not laid back attitude. Retain an 'edge' but avoid undue nervousness. Examinations can be exhilarating if taken as the culmination of hard work and planning. Do not build up thoughts of them in such a way that they become a mental barrier.

The remaining chapters deal with substantive issues of the law of succession. They will serve as an introduction to your studies and an aid to your revision when you can see the subject as a whole.

Remember that the end is but the beginning. Your primary goal at this stage is to pass the course. Your aim in your studies is to become a good lawyer. One hopes you have embarked on the long path out of interest. So long as interest remains a driving force enjoyment will follow. Out of interest, enjoyment and application comes reward, not simply financial but the satisfaction that you have made a worthwhile contribution to practice.

THREE

THE CAPACITY TO MAKE A WILL

Mental capacity

The capacity to make a valid will relates to age and intention. Age is easy, a person must be aged eighteen or over at the date of execution of the will unless the testator comes within privileged status (see chapter 4). The problems under capacity are concerned with the ability to form the intention to make the will. As Shadwell V-C exclaimed 'every testator is free to adopt his own nonsense', *Vaughn* v *Marquis of Headfort* (1840) 10 Sim 639 at 641. Irrationality, eccentricity, may be evidence of a possible problem but they do not in themselves mean that a will would not be admitted to probate. O'Hearn J in *Re Gregory* (1980) 37 NSR (2d) 640 (Canada), pointed out that will making does not require sound judgment; if it did, a great many wills might be ruled to be invalid. One thinks of elderly, wealthy aunts, vacillating over their wills, holding anticipatory relatives on a thread — 'who will she leave it to now?' — as the voice, redolent of Lady Bracknell, thunders 'I think I will go and see Throop, my solicitor, tomorrow . . .'.

The issue of mental capacity is important for it is one fraught with difficulty for the practitioner as well as a favourite area for examiners. Does Throop really know whether Auntie's faculties are failing when she comes along with yet another change of direction?

Keep in mind an overview of the problems which can arise under the general heading of 'capacity'. Firstly there is the general question of mental capacity, simply, did the testator have the requisite capacity when he executed the will? This encompasses evidence of mental illness, burdens of proof, the problems of delusions and the practical problems relating to powers of attorney and registration with the Court of Protection. Secondly there is the broad heading of 'knowledge and approval'. Yes, the testator has the capacity, however, are there vitiating circumstances which impinge upon his ability to form the *animus testandi*? This heading includes suspicion, undue influence, fraud and cases of mistake. Mistake may relate simply to persons executing the wrong document, as in the case of the sisters in *Estate of Meyer* [1908] P 353 or the more difficult mistake as to content.

The test in Banks v Goodfellow

Let us return, however, to the world of eccentricity, irrationality and mental illness. The classic test as to the acceptability of a will, where doubt has been cast as to the ability to form the *animus testandi*, is the dictum of Cockburn CJ in *Banks* v *Goodfellow* (1870) LR 5 QB 549. When he said that the testator must have sound mind, memory and understanding, what did Cockburn CJ mean? By referring to sound mind Cockburn CJ is saying — well, the testator is about to execute his will, does he appreciate it is a will? Does he know he is setting down what should happen to his property on his death? Round J expressed this point well in *Leger* v *Poirier* [1944] 3 DLR 1 (Canada) '. . . a disposing mind . . . is one able to comprehend of its own initiative and volition the essential elements of will making . . .'.

Cockburn CJ said that the testator must understand the extent of the property at his disposal. This does not mean he must be capable of listing every item. Clients, in giving instructions for their wills, sometimes provide a detailed list of all their assets. This is not necessary save in the case of specific legacies. However, the testator should know whether he is wealthy or of modest means. He should be aware of the main assets of the estate and a fair idea of their value. Lack of awareness of a substantial asset can be a warning sign of a decline in faculties.

Finally Cockburn CJ said that the testator must be able to comprehend and appreciate the claims to which he ought to give effect. This is interesting for, as we see in chapter 7, English law has opted for freedom of testamentary disposition in choosing beneficiaries. The constraint in this freedom of choice is the range of potential claimants under the Inheritance (Provision for Family and Dependants) Act 1975 whereby failure to make adequate provision for a surviving spouse or others close to the deceased and dependent upon the deceased, can result in a claim against the estate. However, as a preliminary point, failure to provide for someone whom one would normally expect to be included in the distribution could be an indication of a decline in mental faculties. A good illustration is *Battan Singh* v *Amirchand* [1948] AC 161 where the respondents, instrumental in arranging for the dying testator to see a solicitor to make his last will, failed to remind the testator of a nephew, close to the testator, who would have been a principal beneficiary if the testator had been in possession of his faculties.

In *Banks* v *Goodfellow* (1870) itself the court had to consider whether a person with a known history of suffering from delusions (he thought he was being pursued by the evil spirits of someone long since dead) could make a valid will. The court at first instance emphasised that the time to apply the test is at the time the will is executed. A person suffering from a delusion is considered to be partially of unsound mind in that a delusion is a belief in something which, given the facts and circumstances, no reasonable person would believe. The issue of partial unsoundness had not been considered by the courts before and, in a long judgment Cockburn CJ reviewed the authorities and formulated the three point test.

The measure of capacity

Difficult problems occur where there may be no known history of mental disorder but due to a combination of old age and illness there is a decline in faculties. Several decisions have made the point (and bearing in mind judges need not retire until attaining 75) that old age alone is no bar to making a will(!). However, old age coupled with an illness can cause problems where one may be faced with the fine line between eccentricity and irrationality.

The problem in practice is that although Cockburn CJ's judgment gives the three point test, there is no sliding scale of capacity where one can key in a series of facts and a red or green light appears indicating invalidity as opposed to ability to execute a valid document. What can one do? Capacity must be measured in relation to the facts and subject matter in each case. Was the testator wealthy? Was he or she a worldly person? How old was the testator at the date of the will? Is there evidence of a recent illness? What were the circumstances surrounding the giving of the instructions and the subsequent execution of the will?

Compare the capacity required to make a valid will with the capacity to make other forms of disposition or transactions. For example, compare will making with a gift *inter vivos* or entering the contract of marriage. In *Re Beaney* [1978] 2 All ER 595 the court considered the capacity required to make a gift *inter vivos*, and said that one has to measure the value and extent of the subject matter of the gift as against the remainder of the estate. In no way is the test as stringent as that of will making where the gift is modest in relation to the value of the remainder of the assets of the donor. However, where the subject matter forms a substantial part of the value of the estate, here a house, then the test for capacity is similar to that required to make a will.

An interesting comparison was drawn in the case of will making and the marriage contract in the case of *Estate of Park (dec'd)* [1954] P 112. Here you should note the strategy of the widow, the second wife, in seeking to overturn the complicated will made at the time of the marriage on the basis that she would be entitled to take far more on the ensuing intestacy. A counter argument was provided by a nephew who claimed that if his uncle did not have the capacity to make a valid will, he did not have the capacity to marry: therefore the second wife could not be a wife and thus not a widow! The Court of Appeal equated capacity to marry with the mental capacity required to make a simple will. Here, however, in view of the complicated provisions, the court ruled that, though validly married, the testator lacked the capacity to make such a complex will.

The burden of proof

In practice the difficulty in any challenge to the validity of a will is proof. The persons who are often in a strong position are the proving executors who would move quickly to obtain the grant. Tactically, in mounting a challenge, the person raising doubt should seek to switch the burden of proof to the personal representatives. This is not easy where the will appears rational on the face, for the court will presume capacity unless the challenger can deduce some evidence of lack of capacity, such as prior mental instability, to switch the burden. *Banks* v *Goodfellow* (1870) itself is authority for the presumption of continuance of mental state; therefore where there is evidence of mental illness the burden could move to those who are seeking to prove the will. However, where the testator had the requisite capacity prior to execution there is a presumption of capacity at the time of execution, see, for example, *Chambers and Yatman* v *Queen's Proctor* (1840) 2 Curt 415 where, despite earlier history of mental disorder the court accepted that the will was executed in a period of continuing lucidity.

In the case of the professionally drawn will *Parker* v *Felgate* (1883) 8 PD 171 says that where the testator had the requisite capacity when he gave the instructions for the will, but lacked capacity at the time of execution, the will could still be good. The court must be satisfied that at the time of execution the testator was aware of having given instructions for the will and reasonably believed the will was in accordance with those instructions. Clearly this rule is to be applied with caution. The key to applying the principle in *Parker* v *Felgate* (1883) is proof that the testator knows that he is executing a will about which he has given instructions to a solicitor even though, at the time of execution, he could not understand the will clause by clause. See the dictum of Slade J in *Re Flynn (dec'd)* [1982] 1 All ER 882 at 890.

What steps should be considered at the time of the execution of the will where it is believed that on the death of the testator a challenge may be mounted on the grounds of lack of capacity? A memorandum prepared by the solicitor charged with the preparation of the will would be helpful. Ideally, although not easy to arrange in practice, one should obtain the signatures of medical practitioners as witnesses. See the dictum of Templeman J in *Kenward* v *Adams, The Times*, 29 November 1975 applied by the same judge in *Re Simpson* (1977) 121 SJ 224.

The courts have recognised in cases of known mental disorder that the testator may, at the time of signing the will, do so in a 'lucid interval' as in *Cartwright* v *Cartwright* (1793) 1 Phill 90 where the clear wording and lucidity of the will persuaded the court; and in *Chambers and Yatman* v *Queen's Proctor* (1840) where the evidence showed that the testator was quite rational at the time of execution of the will. Known irrationality may only affect a part of the will. In cases where the testator is suffering from a delusion it is possible to uphold the will or a codicil by excluding the part affected by the irrational belief, so long as what is left makes sense and is untainted by any irrationality. A good example is *Re Bohrmann* [1938] 1 All ER 271 where a later codicil was disregarded as being founded upon an irrational belief.

The question 'does the testator have the requisite capacity?' is not an easy one to answer. The problems in practice are not simply confined to cases of known mental disorder but arise where, say, old age coupled with a recent illness raises doubts about capacity. In *Re Nightingale* (1974) 119 SJ 189 the testator was suffering from a form of cancer which restricted the flow of oxygen to the brain. As a result the testator began to believe, quite irrationally, that his adopted son was trying to shorten his life. Shortly before his death that testator executed a will disinheriting the son. The court refused probate on the grounds of lack of testamentary capacity.

Practical problems

One difficulty with the onset of old age is where the testator does not want to be fussed with the day to day minutiae of investments, signing transfers relating to stock or bank accounts, building societies or rights issues and appoints someone, often a close relative, to deal with such matters under a general power of attorney. The donor of the power must be aware of the effect of the appointment at the time of signing. At this stage there is also no problem about executing a will. What happens, however, if mental capacity declines? Not only would the donor lack the requisite capacity within the test in *Banks* v *Goodfellow* (1870) to make a new will, but the power of attorney is revoked for it is founded upon continuance of mental state. In order to continue with the operation of the day to day business affairs, registration of the donor as a patient with the Court of Protection would be necessary. Two statutory provisions provide assistance where there is a decline in understanding.

The Enduring Powers of Attorney Act 1985 enables an attorney to be appointed who can continue to act under the power when the appointor no longer has the requisite capacity. The appointor must have the capacity at the time of the appointment and be able to appreciate the effect of the power. The power must be in the form prescribed by the Act. Later, when the appointee believes the appointor lacks capacity the power must be registered with the Court of Protection and notice given to the relatives. The advantage of this form of power is the maintenance of continuity in dealing with the donor's affairs. Under a general power, that is, not in the form prescribed by the Act, lack of capacity would bring down the shutters, causing a hiatus until registration with the Court of Protection and the appointment of a receiver to the affairs of the patient. The use instead of the power under the 1985 Act prevents the hiatus and consequential delay in dealing with the assets.

What about the situation where there is a change in the assets of a person who, through a decline in faculties, would be ruled incapable of making a new will? The person may have inherited substantial assets, or changes in taxation may make it desirable to consider a change in the person's will. Statutory powers to enable a will to be made for a patient were enacted in 1968 and are now contained in ss. 93-96 of the Mental Health Act 1983. Under these provisions the Court of Protection can authorise a person to make a will on behalf of a patient; the court must approve the form of the will and, in addition to the requirements as to form in s. 9, Wills Act 1837, the will must be sealed by the court.

In considering the use of these practical steps in any question the patient-testator must still be alive! Read the question carefully! The approach to the formulation and execution of the statutory will were considered in detail by Megarry V-C in *Re D (J)* [1982] Ch 237. An interesting application of the powers was made in *Re C, The Independent*, 2 May 1991, where the court authorised the making of a will on behalf of a patient aged 75, mentally disabled and, since the age of 10, blind. The patient had always been incapable of looking after herself. She had been cared for in hospital and visited by a voluntary helper over the past six years. The patient had assets of £1.6 million inherited from her parents. In view of the patient's condition from the age of 10, there was no information which could provide a guide as to the form of any dispositions which the patient may have wanted. The court ordered a distribution of legacies (in favour of the visitor and the hospital), and division of the remainder as if on intestacy on the basis of the standards of a normal, decent person acting in accordance with prevailing standards of morality.

All human life is here

Issues of morality and questionable behaviour were raised in another case which involved the use of the statutory will, which we can describe as 'the Davey Saga'. The events are a good example of how the law student should respond in applying knowledge of the subject where a point is decided which has implications elsewhere. In *Re Roberts* [1978] 3 All ER 225 the court held that a voidable marriage revoked a will under s. 18, Wills Act 1837 (see chapter 5). This decision flashed a warning light of a possible gap which could occur in the distribution of property on death. A marriage is voidable, inter alia, where one party lacks mental capacity at the time of the marriage. A voidable marriage is one that is valid until avoided. Following *Re Roberts* (1978), if such a marriage revoked any previous will, the testator as party to the marriage could not make a new will, for this would be challenged for want of capacity, nor presumably be able to make a will in contemplation of marriage. The significance of the gap thus created did not take long in coming to court. The case of *Re Davey* [1980] 3 All ER 342 serves as a good illustration of circumstance and human nature. The testatrix, aged 93, resident in a nursing home, made a will in favour of various relatives. Some months later she was registered as a patient with the Court of Protection. A relative, in the course of checking through papers belonging to the testatrix, discovered a marriage certificate showing that the testatrix had entered into a clandestine marriage with Davey, a 48 year old employee of the home, one month after executing the will. The decision of the court in *Re Roberts* (1978) meant that the marriage revoked the will therefore a large part of the estate would pass to Davey on intestacy. The relatives, assisted by solicitors, moved quickly and registered a statutory will following the terms of the last will executed by the testatrix. When the testatrix died, Davey sought unsuccessfully to overturn the statutory will on the basis that he should have been given notice of the application. See the rejoinder by Fox J in answer to protestations by the widower, that he could always apply for family provision! Whether he would have succeeded is another matter!

Knowledge and approval

The issue of testamentary capacity goes beyond mental illness and a failing of faculties. The court must be satisfied that the will reflects the freely formed last wishes of the testator, and that the testator knew the will to be a fair reflection of those wishes. The topic encompasses suspicious circumstances surrounding the preparation and execution of the will, undue influence, fraud and mistake. The cornerstone is the requirement of knowledge and approval on the part of the testator and the propositions laid down by Lord Penzance in *Guardhouse* v *Blackburn* (1866) LR 1 PD 109. Execution by the testator of a will expressed in a rational form is prima facie evidence of knowledge and approval unless evidence can be adduced of suspicion. Evidence that the will was read over to the testator at the time of execution will not necessarily be conclusive. The court will ask who read it over, the testator or someone else; was it a careful reading or a mere cursory glance? Study the dictum of Latey J in *Re Morris* [1970] 1 All ER 1057, a case on mistake.

Suspicion

The classic definition of suspicious circumstances is by Parke B in *Barry* v *Butlin* (1838) 12 ER 1089. The suspicion of the court will be aroused where the will leaves property to someone instrumental in the preparation of the will, as in *Fulton* v *Andrew* (1875) 7 HL 448; and persuasion coupled with a ready prepared will for signing as in *Tyrrell* v *Painton* (1894) P 151. A good illustration of the vigilance of the court can be seen in the judgment in *Re Ticehurst, The Times*, 6 March 1973. The testatrix, aged 82, and given to a vacillating nature, had by earlier wills left certain properties to the sitting tenants. The last will left these properties to nephews. The will was prepared by solicitors but through the means of an intermediary, the wife of one of the nephews. The reason given for the use of an intermediary was the testatrix's failing eyesight. The court rejected the claim that the niece-in-law was a mere go-between, the air of suspicion given the change in direction in the last will was too great.

An even stronger line is adopted where the will leaves benefits to a solicitor who has acted for the testator. The House of Lords agreed with the challenge mounted in person by Colonel Wintle against his aunt's solicitor, Nye in *Wintle* v *Nye* [1959] 1 WLR 284. The House of Lords emphasised the heavy burden of proof which needed to be discharged in such circumstances. Since *Wintle* v *Nye*, following the decision in *Re A Solicitor* [1974] 3 All ER 853, the Law Society has issued guidelines regarding benefits to solicitors. Where the proposed gift is substantial it is not sufficient to show that the client has been asked to seek independent advice but the solicitor must ensure that the client sought independent advice and assistance. What amounts to a substantial gift is left to the facts of each individual case. The lack of a clear *animus* may arise where the testator is suffering from some disability, temporary or permanent, such as the effects of drugs or alcohol, or the testator may be blind. The court will look for evidence surrounding the execution of the will to show that there was understanding on the part of the testator.

Undue influence

Undue influence in the law of wills relates to pressure which changes the direction and intent of the testator. This is not the same as undue influence in the law of contract. The law of wills allows any amount of importuning. Wealthy uncle asks you to witness his will. You protest as he turns and mounts the stairs to the library — 'but Uncle, I am studying this course as part of my law studies and I have read that if a person witnesses a will that person cannot take a benefit under the will'. 'I know' says Uncle. So you cling to Uncle's shins as he climbs the stairs pleading with him. This is not undue influence (although no doubt painful for the uncle) as the law allows any amount of importuning. However, exert pressure, be it physical or mental, which causes a change of direction against the will of the testator, then you have undue influence. Defined by Lord Penzance in *Hall* v *Hall* (1868) LR 1 P&D 481, he points out the testator may be led but not driven. 'Influence may be degrading and pernicious and yet not undue influence in the eyes of the law' said Lord Macnaghten in *Boudains* v *Richardson* (1906).

Clearly where there is evidence of coercion or violence, undue influence would be proved. More difficult are the situations where an individual is in a position to exert pressure on the mind of the other. The burden of proof rests with the person making the allegation. It is not sufficient to show that the person was in a position to exert influence, the evidence must show that influence has been exercised and that the contents of the will are based upon that influence.

Fraud

In order to set aside a will on the grounds of fraud the person alleging fraud must actually prove deceit. There are few reported cases. For example, inserting a clause before execution without the knowledge of the testator, or pretending clauses being read to the testator are in the will when they are not, would amount to fraud. False representations as to status or character may amount to fraud; see *Wilson* v *Joughlin* (1866) where a woman falsely represented herself as single, entered into a bigamous marriage and encouraged the testator to leave to her property in his will. The gift was set aside.

In problem questions look for evidence of factors which could lead to a conclusion that the testator lacked the necessary knowledge and approval at the time of the execution of the will. Look at the state of health and mind of the testator; the circumstances surrounding the preparation of the will; the relationship of the beneficiary to the deceased. Couple this with the general test encompassed by the three questions asked by Cockburn CJ in *Banks* v *Goodfellow* (1870).

Mistake

Mistake is a broader category whereby in a number of situations one can say the testator lacked the necessary testamentary intent, the *animus testandi*. The cases range over a number of situations, from the simple execution of the wrong document as in *Estate of Meyer* [1908] P 353, to the more difficult areas of mistake as to meaning of the words used and clerical error.

In the case of mistake as to the words used there is a fine line between mistake as to meaning and mistake as to legal effect. The case of *Collins* v

Elstone [1893] P 1 needs to be carefully studied. Here, a revocation clause which the testatrix did not intend was left in the will when she was mis-informed as to its effect. The decision has been criticised, for, in letting the clause stand, one could not say that the testatrix knew and approved of the contents. Further, should the situation arise today two possible courses of action may be open. First, the limited right to obtain rectification of the will under s. 20 of the Administration of Justice Act 1982; and secondly, action against professional advisers for mis-information under the principle in *Ross* v *Caunters* [1980] Ch 297. A good example of a case where the court concluded that the testator did not apply his mind at all to the inclusion of printed revocation clauses in a series of will forms, all executed on the same day, is *Re Phelan* (1972) Fam 33.

Difficulties have been caused by cases of clerical error. Two good examples are *Re Morris* [1970] 1 All ER 1057 and *Re Reynette-James* [1975] 3 All ER 1037. What can the court do when faced with a clear case of clerical error? Words or phrases could be omitted on the ground of lack of knowledge or approval (not an easy line, as shown by *Collins* v *Ellstone* (1893)); reference could be made to the court as a court of construction to try to determine what should have been written (see the judgment in *Re Morris* (1970)) and, in the case of deaths after 31 December 1982, use could be made of the statutory power to rectify under s. 20 of the Administration of Justice Act 1982. Note, however, that the statutory power is limited to clerical error and a failure to understand instructions given by a client. The section will not apply where there has been a failure to carry out the instructions of the testator, for example, by understanding the instructions yet consciously omitting a legacy or giving misleading advice as to the effect of a clause.

In *Wordingham* v *Royal Exchange Trust Co. Ltd and another* [1992] 3 All ER 204 the court construed 'clerical error' in s. 20(1)(a) of the 1982 Act to mean an inadvertent error made in the process of recording the intended words of the testator in the drafting or transcription of his will. This is to be contrasted with an error made in carrying the testator's intentions into effect by the draftsman's choice of words, and with a mistaken choice of words because of a failure to understand the testator's intentions. In the case of a failure to understand instructions rectification would be possible under s. 20(1)(b). Here, rectification of the will of the testatrix to include the exercise of a power of appointment in favour of the plaintiff husband was ordered on the basis that the mistake did not arise from any misunderstanding by the solicitor draftsman as to the nature of the instructions. This was a mechanical error in preparing a draft altered will. Evans-Lombe QC in his judgment added that if the power to rectify did not arise from his construction of s. 20(1)(a), then he would be minded to strike out the whole will for want of knowledge and approval on the part of the testatrix; for the exercise of the power of appointment constituted a large part of the income for her and her beneficiary husband.

The courts are quick to point out the possibility that the beneficiaries could sue the solicitors responsible for the preparation of the will in negligence on the authority of *Ross* v *Caunters* (1980). Here, solicitors were held liable under the general principles of negligence in failing to give clearer instructions concerning the execution of a will, with the result that a benefit was denied through the operation of s. 15, Wills Act 1837. The court held that the duty of care was owed not only to the testator but to the beneficiaries expecting to take a benefit on the death of the testator. Limitations upon the extent of the principle in *Ross* v *Caunters* (1980) were considered by the Court of Appeal in *Clarke* v *Bruce, Lance & Co. (a firm)* [1988] 1 All ER 364 where no duty of care was owed to a beneficiary under the will of the testator in relation to advice concerning an option granted by the testator which reduced one of the assets in the estate. Here, the duty was owed to the testator alone and did not extend to potential beneficaries.

Subsequently doubts about the decision in *Ross* v *Caunters* have been expressed in the light of the decisions in negligence in *Caparo Industries plc* v *Dickman* [1990] 1 All ER 568 and *Murphy* v *Brentwood District Council* [1990] 2 All ER 908. However the Court of Appeal in *White* v *Jones, The Times,* 9 March 1993 has stated that *Ross* v *Caunters* is still good law. Here, a testator disinherited two daughters following a family row. Later there was a reconciliation and the testator gave instructions to solicitors to draft a new will leaving legacies of £9,000 each to the daughters. The solicitors were negligent in their delay and the testator died before the will was prepared. The court held that it was clearly foreseeable to the solicitors that if they failed to prepare the will, in accordance with the instructions, the beneficiaries would suffer loss. The issue turned upon proximity and whether it was fair to impose a duty. A central point in the case was that since the testator was under no duty to confer a gratuitous benefit on his intended beneficiaries, there was no reason to impose on the testator's professional adviser a duty which went further than that on the testator.

In general a solicitor owed a professional duty of care to his client and to no one else. However, Nichols V-C said that instructions to prepare a will were different from other instructions to a solicitor. The failure to carry them out properly resulted in the client's purpose being thwarted but left the client with no effective remedy. In these circumstances the solicitor should be liable to the third party. This was sufficient proximity to create a special relationship between the solicitor and the intended beneficiary thereby making the matter actionable where loss had occurred.

FOUR

FORMAL VALIDITY

Introduction

This is a popular topic for examination purposes. At first glance the requirements of the valid execution of a will appear straightforward, but when one studies the statutory provisions and considers the cases, born out of human foibles and error, tricky situations emerge. There are a number of threads which run through the material on formal validity: e.g., the ghost of the Statute of Frauds of 1677, the Law Commission Report 'The making and revocation of wills', Cmnd 7902 (1980) and the re-writing of s. 9, Wills Act 1837 by s. 17, Administration of Justice Act 1982.

What do the threads tell us? The Statute of Frauds was concerned with, as its title suggests, protection against fraud. The disposition of property on death is an important step. Just as in chapter 3 you saw that the law seeks to ensure that testamentary intention is freely formed and if not will refuse to admit the will, so statute is concerned that the form of the disposition should give some protection against fraud. Hence, in the signing of the will by the testator there is the basic requirement that the testator should sign the will in the presence of two witnesses who are not beneficiaries under the will. The provisions were modified by s. 9, Wills Act 1837 but are built upon the same principle. Since the passing of the Wills Act a long list of case authorities has built up on the interpretation of signature, acknowledgement and presence. In their report of 1980 the Law Commission sought a balance between protection against fraud and purely mechanical failure, that is, where strict adherence to the letter of s. 9 has not been followed, although there is no suggestion of fraud, but the will is declared invalid for non-compliance of form. A good illustration, highlighted by the Law Commission, was the decision in *Re Colling* [1972] 3 All ER 729. The facts could have been made for the examination room. The testator was in a hospital bed signing his will in the presence of two witnesses when one witness was called away and, when the witness returned, the testator and the other witness had signed the will. Although the second witness then added his name, the will failed for non-compliance with s. 9. Consider for yourself what the parties should have done when the witness returned to the bedside and then look again at the case by applying the amended s. 9, i.e., as it is now to be found in s. 17 of the Administration of Justice Act 1982. A thorough understanding of s. 9, Wills Act 1837 is important. Study the amended section line by line. In this chapter the way to approach formal validity is considered but it is intended to be complementary to a thorough study of the section and related cases.

Formal requirements

Writing

The will must be in writing, type written or ink is preferred: the courts consider writing in pencil to be merely deliberative. What about the impact of modern technology? What about the taped will or the video will with the testator presenting his own last wishes? The courts are unlikely to accept an interpretation of s. 9 of the 1837 Act which would extend 'writing' to these methods. The 1980 report of the Law Commission (Cmnd 7902) rejected the idea, recognised by some Canadian and US authorities, of an informal holograph will supported by testamentary intention.

Signature

'Signature' has been widely interpreted as in *Re Cook* [1960] 1 All ER 689 where a letter signed 'your loving mother' was held to be valid, and *In the Goods of Sperling* [1863] 3 Sw & Tr 272 where the signature of a witness to the will took the form of a job description. What has caused difficulty has been the position of the signature. Here again note the pull in interpretation between guarding against fraud and trying to avoid mere mechanical failure. After the passing of the 1837 Act concern grew over the number of wills failing on the strict interpretation of the words 'foot or end thereof'. To counter this, the Wills Act Amendment Act 1852 was passed. This sought to create greater flexibility in the signing of the will, see, for example, *Re Hornby* [1946] P 171. However, the main aim was to protect against fraud so nothing following the signature was admissible, see *Re Stalman* [1931] All ER Rep. 193 where a will signed at the top of the single page, when there was no room at the foot, was declared invalid. The court rejected an argument based upon the end in time in favour of 'end' meaning the physical end of the will. In cases where the testator has signed more than once look for the operative signature, that is, the signature which the testator intended as the execution of his will and ask to have the witnesses attested to that signature, see, for example, *Re Bercovitz* [1962] 1 All ER 552.

The Administration of Justice Act 1882 repealed the Wills Act Amendment Act 1852 and it refers to the signature whereby the testator 'intends to give effect to . . .' (the will). The change has been tested by the decision in *Wood* v *Smith* [1992] 3 All ER 556 where the testator commenced his will 'I Percy Winterborne of . . .'. He did not sign at the end of the will and, when a witness pointed out that he had not signed, he replied 'yes I have, I have signed at the top', adding the (ominous) words 'it can be signed anywhere'. Study the report and see how counsel for the beneficiaries argued that the signing and dispositions were all part of one transaction. Consider the implications of this argument.

The Court of Appeal stated the signature (which could be a written name) did not necessarily have to be appended to the document *after* the substantive testamentary contents had been written on the document in order to satisfy the requirements of s. 9(b), provided the writing of the will, and the appending of the signature, were all in one operation. The court concluded that s. 9 had been satisfied. However, the court refused to admit the will to probate on the basis that the testator had failed the test as to capacity within *Banks* v *Goodfellow* (1870).

The primary purpose of s. 9, Wills Act 1837 is to prevent fraud. Emphasis was placed upon the signature and dispositions being all in one operation. Scott LJ cited Park QC (sitting as a Deputy Judge) in *Re White (dec'd), Barker* v *Gribble* [1990] 3 All ER 1 where Park QC envisaged the testator signing a blank sheet of paper, then, in a continuing process, writes in, above the signature, the dispositions and then asks two witnesses to attest. This would be admissable. However, where the evidence showed a blank page had been signed by the testator and the dispositions filled in some time later, this would be unacceptable.

Envelopes

A twist (in the sense of 'turn' not 'trick'!) to look for in questions on formal validity is the situation where the testator places the will in an envelope and signs the envelope. Can the envelope together with the paper containing the dispositions be admitted together as a valid will? The key questions here are: (i) where is the operative signature of the testator? and (ii) is that signature attested? Note the approach and review of the cases in *Re Beadle* [1974] 1 All ER 493. Spot the grammatical error by Mr Mayes in his writing on the envelope!

By way of illustration let us consider the will of George. He wrote his will on the back of an envelope and signed it 'Pops'. He then called his neighbours Fred and Ann into the room and, pointing to the envelope, said, 'here, look, I want you to put your names to this'. Fred signed the envelope below the word 'Pops'. There was no more room so Ann signed on the back of the envelope. Had the will been validly executed?

George does not have to sign his name, any signing will suffice so long as it can be identified as his signature. He acknowledged his signing in the presence of Fred and Ann. As attesting witnesses they can sign the will where they like, so long as it is clear that they are attesting to the signature by George. The Wills Act 1837 is not prescriptive as to where the witnesses sign. The will would be admissible to probate. Where the testator has signed more than once, then evidence must be adduced as to which signature the witnesses attested, which brings one back to the judgment in *Re Beadle* (1974).

Acknowledgement

A point which often causes confusion is that the testator need not sign in the presence of the witnesses. He could have signed the will earlier, quite alone, so long as he subsequently acknowledges his signature in the presence of the witnesses. The role of the witnesses is to attest to the fact of the testator's signature. It follows therefore that the witnesses must be able to see the signature.

Picture the scene: Two friends, we'll call them Danny and Peter, are chatting over coffee when another friend, the houseowner, Ed, enters the room wearing an overcoat. Ed taps the overcoat and says 'I've got my will here which I have signed, will you witness it, please'. He then leaves the room and crosses to the dining room to say hello to his parrot, Arnold. Danny enters the room. Ed takes the will out of his pocket, points to it and Danny signs. Danny then leaves the room as Peter, who has been finishing his drink enters the room. Danny says 'He is talking to that parrot again'. Peter then signs the will as the second witness. Has the will been validly executed? Ed had signed the will sometime before seeing Danny and Peter. This is acceptable so long as Ed acknowledges his signature in the presence of the two witnesses. Has there been a valid acknowledgement? The answer is 'no'. When Ed first entered the room where the friends were having a drink the will was still in his coat pocket. Although all three were present and Ed referred to his will, Danny and Peter could not see the will, or more particularly, the signature. When the will is eventually produced in the dining room, under the beady eye of Arnold, only one witness was present at any one time when a valid acknowledgement could be made, for Danny had left the room before Peter entered, and parrots cannot witness wills. The scenario, with a little poetic licence, is based upon *Re Groffman* [1969] 2 All ER 108. Both witnesses must be in a position to see the signature when the testator acknowledges. In the *Goods of Gunstan* (1882) 7 PD 102 the will failed where the signature of the testator had been covered over by blotting paper. In *Re Groffman* counsel argued that the witnesses in *Gunstan* could have seen the signature if they had asked to do so. This argument was

rejected in *Re Groffman* for, if they had done so, *Gunstan* would have gone
the other way. Counsel in *Re Groffman* sought to distinguish *Gunstan* on the
ground that in *Gunstan* the testator had deliberately concealed his signature
but this line was rejected for there was no suggestion that active concealment
formed part of the ratio of *Gunstan*.

Witnesses

The role of the witnesses is to attest to a signing or an acknowledgement. It
follows therefore that the attestation must be after the act of signing or
acknowledging by the testator. Under the original wording of s. 9, Wills Act
1837 a witness could not acknowledge his signature to the testator, see for
example *Wyatt* v *Berry* [1893] P 5. Under the revised s. 9 a witness can either
sign or acknowledge provided this is done in the presence of the testator. A
way to understand the change is to consider what the first witness in *Re
Colling* (1972) supra, should do if the facts occurred post 1982. The witness
would not have to sign again but could acknowledge the signature already
made.

Presence

The word 'presence' in s. 9 denotes both a physical and a mental presence.
Problem questions on formal validity frequently describe a scenario where
the witnesses take the will to an adjoining office or to a part of the room
which is partially screened. The key here is in asking the question 'could the

Signed in the presence of

testator have seen the witnesses sign if he had wanted to?' In other words you do not have to prove that the testator actually saw the witnesses sign, but you must be able to prove that the line of sight was such that the testator could have seen. This is well illustrated by contrasting the old cases of *Casson* v *Dade* (1781) 1 Bro CC 99 and *Shires* v *Glascock* (1688) 2 Salk 688 with *Norton* v *Bazett* (1856) Dea & Sw 259.

In *Brown* v *Skirrow* [1902] P 3 the testatrix took her will into the local shop to have it witnessed! The two assistants were serving at counters at either end of the shop. The testatrix signed in the presence of the first assistant whilst the second assistant was busy serving a customer. The first assistant then attested and the testatrix asked the second assistant to attest. The will failed for, at the time of the signing by the testatrix, the second assistant could not see what was happening even if she had looked up from her serving. Presence also denotes a mental presence, i.e., an awareness of what is happening. See dicta in *the Goods of Chalcraft* [1948] 1 All ER 700; the case is also a good authority on the signing of the will.

Do the witnesses have to sign in the presence of one another? No. Section 9, Wills Act 1837 states '. . . and no form of attestation shall be necessary'. The essentials to keep in mind, as a problem is analysed, are the testator signing or acknowledging in the presence of the two witnesses present at the same time and, on attestation, each witness signs in the presence of the testator. However, on a practical note, if the 'standard form' attestation clause is not used, the court will call for further proof (usually by means of the affidavit of due execution sworn, where possible, by the witnesses). The 'standard form' clause, so-called because it is the common precedent clause used for the execution of wills, requires the witnesses to sign, not only in the presence of the testator, but also in the presence of each other. The use of the standard form clause removes the need for further proof unless there is evidence adduced which puts the court on suspicion. In *Re Bercovitz* [1962] 1 All ER 552, for example, the signature of the testator appeared twice, once at the top and again at the foot of the will. The affidavit evidence of the witnesses showed that they had attested the signature at the top, therefore the will was inadmissible to probate.

The witness as beneficiary — bad news!

Under the Statute of Frauds 1677 witnesses to the will had to be 'credible'. If a witness or the spouse of the witness was a beneficiary, the whole will failed. This hard stance was modified by s. 15, Wills Act 1837 which denies the benefit to the witness or spouse in those circumstances so that the gift lapses but the will does not fail. This provision should be borne in mind in questions on other areas of the subject, for example, in the case of a witness who is a residuary beneficiary, the share of that beneficiary would lapse and, in the absence of a gift over, could cause a partial intestacy.

The courts consider the rule in s. 15 to be harsh and have tended to construe the section narrowly. In *Thorpe v Bestwick* (1881) 6 QBD 311 the testator made a will leaving certain property to a spinster, X. After the will but before the death of the testator a witness to the will married X. The gift was effective. Further, if the beneficiary witnesses the will and the will is later confirmed by a codicil which the beneficiary does not witness, the beneficiary can take by reference to the codicil, as in *Anderson v Anderson* (1872) LR 13 Eq 381. Also a narrow construction was adopted in *Gurney v Gurney* (1855) 3 Drew 208 where a residuary beneficiary witnessed a codicil revoking a legacy thereby indirectly increasing the value of the residue: s. 15 was not invoked.

However, the trap of s. 15 remains despite the courts' narrow construction, as shown in *Re Bravda* [1968] 2 All ER 217. The unfortunate events in *Re Bravda* led to the passing of the Wills Act 1968 whereby the court has power to disregard the attestation of a witness if the will would still be validly executed under s. 9, Wills Act 1837 without that witness.

Rider

Although many of the cases you refer to in studying this topic are old and appear well settled, the situations testators create for themselves in modern settings, such as *Re Groffman*, show that it is still easy to fall foul of s. 9, Wills Act 1837. A situation which did not come before the courts for, happily, the lady survived, is where a widow, about to embark on a flight to a holiday destination, the first after the death of her husband, spent a large part of the evening before departure writing out her will, assisted by her daughter and son-in-law to whom she was close. At the end of the evening the will form (!), which referred to, '. . . all my moneys . . .' (!), leaving the bulk of her estate to her daughter, was witnessed by — yes — you have guessed — the daughter and son-in-law!

Privileged wills

This is a topic of intermittent popularity on degree papers although of only passing note in professional course, but one that gives pleasure in lecturing and some enjoyment, if that is the right word, in revision. However, do not make the common mistake of thinking that because it is enjoyable to revise it is necessarily going to come up, therefore, when it does not, you are determined to get it into an answer in any event! Privilege covers situations when a testator can make an effective testamentary disposition without any formalities whatsoever. The will could, therefore, be oral and still admissible, as in *Re Jones (dec'd)* (1981) Fam 7, so long as there is proof of evidence.

The acid test as to when privileged status can be claimed relates to the circumstances prevailing at the time when the will is made and not the circumstances of death. The key to this topic is in understanding the situations which amount to privileged status: these are to be found in two terms within s. 11, Wills Act 1837, namely, 'actual military service' and 'any mariner at sea'. 'Actual military service' has been defined as 'active military service'. The leading judgment is that of Bucknell LJ in *Re Wingham* [1948] 2 All ER 908. The principles draw upon the Roman law distinction of 'in garrison' and '*in expeditione*'. When the 20th Legion received its marching orders the senatorial commander would take along not only his foot soldiers; his retinue would include physician, musician, slaves, general entertainment but rarely his lawyer (!) who would plead his pleadings were urgently needed at home! The Romans set great store by the concept of the family and the passing of property on death. Roman law acknowledged the ability to make an informal declaration, even with the blade of the sword writing in blood on the sand, when one was '*in expeditione*'.

In the definition of 'active military service' war need not be in progress, as in *Re Wingham*, but can be imminent or recently concluded as in the interesting case of *Re Colman* [1958] 2 All ER 35.

How does the concept of 'actual military service' apply to the modern role of the armed services in peace-keeping roles or in combating terrorist

and Mavis you can have my boat

activities? *Re Anderson* (1955) allowed a soldier in the Malayan emergency to make an informal declaration. In *Re Jones* [1981] Fam 7 the courts considered the role of the British Army in Northern Ireland. Arnold P, in a judgment allowing admission to probate of a dying soldier's oral declaration, used the phrase 'totality of the environment' in considering whether there is active service and, he added, if there is any doubt, that doubt should be given in favour of validation.

Privileged status also extends to 'any mariner at sea'. This is clearly a wider concept and reflects the hazards of life at sea. This category has received a wide interpretation by the courts. The term 'mariner' extends to civilian employees of shipping companies as well as the merchantmen who man the ships. 'At sea' has also been given a wide interpretation and the generous approach adopted by the courts to both terms is illustrated by the judgment in *the Goods of Sarah Hale* [1915]. Poor Sarah was a typist employed by the Cunard line. Whilst in lodgings in Southampton prior to embarkation, she wrote to her mother. The letter included certain testamentary wishes. Unfortunately the ship to which Sarah was attached was the ill-fated *'Lusitania'*. The letter was admitted as a will under s. 11. Although the *Hale* case shows you need not be 'at sea' there must be some obligation upon the mariner to join or re-join a particular ship. Hence in *the Estate of Rapley dec'd* [1983] 1 WLR 1069 the informal declaration of a merchant seaman was not privileged where, at the time of the declaration, he had been discharged from one ship and had not signed papers to join another ship within the same company.

Even where it is shown that the person came within privileged status, in order to admit a disposition to probate, there must be testamentary intention. A distinction is drawn between words which convey testamentary intention, for example in *Re Stable* [1919] P 7, and words which are merely imparting information and imply steps which have already been taken to make a testamentary disposition, as in the series of conversations between the two barmen on board the passenger liner *'Arcadia'* in *Re Knibbs* [1962] 2 All ER 829. An interesting line, given the evidence, was taken in the *Goods of Spicer* [1949] P 441, where the court linked the words used with evidence concerning a missing army pay book.

An essay topic in this area of study is to consider critically the need to retain the categories of privilege in this day and age. Remember, where you are asked to 'consider critically' this does mean simply a descriptive account of the law; rather, through your knowledge of s. 11 and the case law, give your comments on the continued justification of this exception to formal validity. Alternatively you may be faced with a problem which asks you to consider one or other of the categories, their meaning and the importance of intention.

Problem

Let us consider friends Alec and Brian, who both join the army. On leave, Alec meets Brian's sister, Rita. They enjoy a brief, passionate affair. On returning to their unit Alec and Brian are posted to Northern Ireland. Four months later Rita writes to Alec saying she is expecting his child. Alec appears reluctant to communicate with Rita and Brian urges him to consider her and the child. Eventually Alec says to Briah 'Ok, you win, I will see her straight'. The next day Alec is fatally wounded. On the way to the hospital Brian asks him 'what are you going to do about Rita?'. Alec, growing weaker by the minute, says 'I am finished for, give it all to Rita'. Alec dies that night. Are the words admissible as a privileged will?

Alec is clearly in military service. Is the service 'actual'? Yes, according to *Re Wingham* (1948) and the totality of the environment test in *Re Jones* (1981). Do the words convey testamentary intent? The words 'Ok, you win, I will see her straight' do not, for they imply a future step to make provision, they lack immediate testamentary intent. However, the words 'I am finished for, give it all to Rita' do convey testamentary intent, applying *Re Stable* (1919) and *Re Jones*.

Finally, note that whilst a testator enjoys privileged status wills can not only be made but can be revoked informally. So, when Jack Tar reaches the end of the plank at the end of the sword blade and falls seaward he can call to Arnold (the parrot again) 'the necklace I left to Esmeralda, I've changed my mind . . .'. Splash. What happens if the words were 'the necklace I left to Esmeralda, I've . . .' splash, is anyone's guess.

Question

'The provisions relating to informal testamentary dispositions are anachronistic and should be repealed.' Discuss.

Comment

The proposition is asking you to explain the provisions in s. 11 of the Wills Act 1837 whereby certain persons can make informal testamentary dispositions, that is, without the strict requirements as to form in s. 9 of the 1837 Act.

The two categories in s. 11 should be considered, namely, any 'soldier being in actual military service' and any 'mariner at sea'. After explaining the meaning and the extent of the two categories there should be a critique whereby you give your view upon the need for the retention of s. 11 either wholly or in part.

Suggested format

Section 11 of the Wills Act 1837 refers to two categories, 'actual military service' and 'any mariner at sea'. Where a person can show he or she came within one of these categories at the time of making a testamentary disposition the strict requirements as to form in s. 9 do not apply and the court will accept an informal, even verbal, disposition, provided the words used convey sufficient testamentary intention.

'Actual military service' has been interpreted as active military service. The leading case on the interpretation is the Court of Appeal decision in *Re Wingham* [1948] 2 All ER 908. The court had to consider the validity of an informal will made by a trainee pilot during the Second World War. The training camp was in Canada, well removed from the theatre of war. However, the court held that Wigham was on active service for he could, at short notice, be ordered to join a squadron in Britain, ready to engage the enemy. The court considered the scope of the phrase 'actual military service' and interpreted it as applying not just during conflict but, in the words of Bucknill LJ, where hostilities were imminent or recently concluded.

In the *Estate of Colman* [1958] 2 All ER 35 the court was prepared to accept a will made by an under-aged soldier who, at the time the will was executed, was serving with the British army in occupation of the Rhineland. The army was still regarded as an army of occupation rather than merely garrisoned for training purposes nine years after the end of the war. The courts have sought to limit the scope of actual military service by drawing upon the Roman law distinction between soldiers who are 'in *expeditione*' as opposed to 'in garrison'; the former being considered able to make an informal disposition.

Is this part of s. 11 justified today given the role of the modern army. The court in *Re Anderson's Will* (1958) 75 WN (NSW) 334 was asked to consider an informal declaration made by an Australian soldier during the Malayan emergency and accepted that the circumstances justified privileged status. Similarly in *Re Berry* [1955] NZLR 1003 privileged status applied to a New Zealand soldier sent to Korea as part of the United Nations forces.

The role of the armed forces in Northern Ireland was considered in *Re Jones* [1981] 1 All ER 1 where a soldier, dying from sniper fire, was held to have made an admissible oral testamentary declaration. Arnold P, after drawing the distinction between garrison duties and 'in *expeditione*' said one has to consider the 'totality of the environment'.

The other limb of s. 11 is 'any mariner at sea'. This is a wider concept. 'Mariner' is not confined to Royal naval personnel but can include merchant seamen. The term 'at sea' does not refer to hostilities, it merely recognises the hostile environment in which those who earn their living by going to sea have to face. The terms 'mariner' and 'at sea' have been widely interpreted.

A good illustration is *Re Hale's Goods* [1915] 2 IR 362 where a typist employed by the Cunard line was held to have made an informal will when writing to her mother from her lodgings in Southampton prior to sailing on the ill-fated liner *Lusitania*. Although the interpretation of this limb of s. 11 appears to be very wide, there must be proof of connection between the testator and the ship. This point is illustrated by *Re Rapley's Estate* [1983] 1 WLR 1069 where the court held privileged status did not extend to a merchant seaman who, at the time of the declaration, was between ships, that is, not contractually bound to a particular ship within the merchant company.

Can one justify the exception to s. 9 formal validity today? In the case of soldiers in actual military service *Re Jones* is a good illustration of the need for the means to make an informal disposition in relation to the policing role of the modern army. In addition action in the South Atlantic and more recently in the Gulf States demonstrates that the role of the soldier, airman and naval personnel is hazardous and justifies the retention. The sea remains a natural hazard and, despite the decline in transport by sea in the latter part of the twentieth century, the exception should remain. Although this part of the section has been widely interpreted, for example, in *Re McMurdo's Goods* (1868) LRIP & D 540 where privilege extended to a sailor serving on a permanently moored ship which never left harbour, the decision in *Re Rapley* does show the court prepared to set some limit by not extending the exception to a sailor on leave.

FIVE

REVOCATION

Introduction

A will is ambulatory, that is, effective upon the happening of an event, i.e., the death of the testator. A will remains revocable until the moment of death. Revocation can occur informally whilst the testator enjoys privileged status, by action of the testator or by operation of law. Revocation by action of the testator is governed by s. 20, Wills Act 1837 and can be express, by the use of a revocation clause; implied, by a later, inconsistent provision or by an act of destruction. Section 18, Wills Act 1837 governs revocation by marriage and divorce.

Suppose our testator, Tom, completes a will form leaving 'The Gables' to Henry. The remainder of his property has been disposed of by an earlier, validly executed will. The will form contains a printed clause expressly revoking all former wills — is he bound by the clause? The clause would have the effect of revoking the earlier will leaving the only valid gift the specific legacy to Henry. Did Tom direct his mind to the clause when he signed the form?

Suppose Tom telephones his solicitor saying he is calling to make a new will. The solicitor asks his clerk, Uriah, to take out the will explaining the reason for Tom's calling. Uriah throws the will onto the fire saying it is no longer needed. Tom dies before he can execute a new will.

Suppose Tom has his original will in his possession and, as he sets out to see his solicitor, crumples the will up and throws it on the desk saying 'this is no longer needed'. Tom dies before he can execute the new will.

Does the will form revoke the earlier will?

Does Uriah revoke Tom's will?

Does Tom himself revoke the will when he throws it on the desk?

Section 20 revocation divides into revocation by later testamentary instruction, and revocation by destruction. Revocation by a later testamentary instrument can either be by express words or by implication.

Express revocation

Express revocation must be by clear words of revocation, for example, 'I hereby revoke all former testamentary instruments heretofore made by me and declare this to be my last will'. Merely describing a document as 'the last will' does not amount to an express revocation (*Kitcat* v *King* [1930] P 266) but could still effect an implied revocation. The words of revocation need not be contained in a will, that is, an instrument containing provisions for disposal, so long as the document is executed in accordance with s. 9, Wills Act 1837. An example is *Re Durance* (1872) LR 2 P&D 406 where the words of revocation were contained in a signed, attested letter, requesting the testator's brother to destroy the testator's will.

How far is the testator bound by an express revocation clause in the document he has signed? *Collins* v *Elstone* [1893] P 1 shows that merely misunderstanding the legal effect will mean that the testator is bound by the clause. Here, the court took the view that the testator knew and approved of the clause. Mistake was unsuccessfully pleaded for the mistake did not relate to the words used, but rather to their legal effect. One could argue that this case is rather harsh in that the testatrix queried the clause and was told that it only applied to an insurance policy, when in fact it applied to all the property in the estate. The issue would today be actionable under the principle in *Ross* v *Caunters* [1979] 3 All ER 580. Contrast the *Collins* case with *Marklew* v *Turner* (1900) 17 TLR 10 where, in making a later codicil, the testator thought it would not be effective without inserting a revocation clause from a precedent. However, the intention of the later will was to supplement the earlier will and the court concluded that both the will and the later codicil should be admitted to probate with the words of revocation omitted from the codicil.

Clearly a heavy burden will fall upon a plaintiff who is asking the court to disregard an express revocation clause, see, for example, the dictum of Langton J in *Lowthorpe-Lutwidge* v *Lowthorpe-Lutwidge* [1935] All ER Rep 338.

The court has disregarded an express revocation clause where there is evidence of a contrary intention; see *Re Wayland* [1951] 2 All ER 1041. Here wills dealing respectively with property in Belgium and England were both admitted to probate despite the later will, which dealt with the English property, containing an express revocation clause.

Consider what is meant by a will. The court does not simply view the single document but looks at all the testamentary instruments collectively to determine the intention of the testator; see, for example, the dictum of Judge Micklem in *Re Finnemore (dec'd)* [1992] 1 All ER 800.

Will forms

The clause can be disregarded for want of knowledge and approval. This is well illustrated by the admission to probate of a series of will forms, all dated on the same day, leaving separate property but each containing express revocation clauses, in *Re Phelan* [1971] 3 WLR 888. Looking at the testamentary intention as a whole, the court accepted that the testator had never applied his mind to the revocation clauses. An express revocation clause can also be disregarded under the doctrine of conditional revocation which is considered later in this chapter.

Implied revocation

A will may be revoked by implication. Since the will represents the last wishes of the testator, one takes the last, validly executed document as admissible to probate. However, if the document does not contain a revocation clause, earlier testamentary documents may be admitted in so far as they are not inconsistent with the later document. If, however, the last admissible document disposes of the whole of the estate, then all previous wills are impliedly revoked. Whether the last will revokes all or a part of the earlier testamentary documents is a matter of construction. The court will look at the substance of the later document to determine the intention of the testator, i.e., to ascertain whether he intended to revoke the earlier documents wholly or in part; see dicta in *Dempsey* v *Lawson* (1877) 2 PD 98.

Questions of revocation by later instruments underlie the importance of dating wills. How can one construe the last wishes of the testator if the court is not sure whether the document in question is the last will? The court has power to call for an affidavit of search (r. 14(4), Non Contentious Probate Rules 1987). *Re Howard* [1944] P 39 is unusual in that the testator had executed two wills dated the same day, both containing revocation clauses and both wholly inconsistent. The court held that the wills were inadmissible to probate as being irreconcilable, but they did provide sufficient evidence to show an intention to revoke an earlier will, therefore the testator died intestate.

Whether the purported revocation is express or implied depends upon the effectiveness of the later instrument. Suppose the revoking instrument fails to take effect either wholly or in part, for example, through incorrect execution contrary to s. 9, Wills Act 1837, or where the attesting witness is a beneficiary or the spouse of the beneficiary (s. 15, Wills Act 1837).

Suppose by his first will Tom gives all his property to Eric. By a later will Tom leaves all his property to Frank. The later will revokes the gift to Eric (*Re Hawksley's Settlement* [1934] Ch 384). Suppose, however, that the will in favour of Frank fails to take effect, perhaps because it has been incorrectly executed. Does this mean that Eric's will is revoked? The House of Lords in *Ward v Van der Loeff* [1924] AC 653, held that it would not be revoked in the absence of any other evidence of a valid intention to revoke; see the dictum of Lord Haldane.

In *Re Robinson* [1930] 2 Ch 332 the testatrix by her will gave her estate on trust to pay an annuity to her son H and after his death to divide the capital between her grandchildren at 21. By a later will she gave her whole estate to H absolutely: the disposition failed because H's wife was an attesting witness. The earlier will was not revoked for, the court concluded, the testatrix had not shown an intention to revoke in any event. The court construed her intention to revoke as conditional upon the absolute gift to H taking effect. The intention to revoke must be as clear as the intention to make the original will.

Testators sometimes attempt to go further in their revocation of a previous bequest by adding that the will is to be construed 'as if the beneficiary were dead'. Why? It is a part of human nature to need to make sure. This approach to revocation is rather like the approach of the person who, prescribed one tablet three times a day, takes six straight off thinking that this will lead to a faster cure. The danger of adopting the heavy handed approach to revocation is that this may not reflect the true intention of the testator. The constructional problem posed by such an approach is seen in *Re Wray* [1951] Ch 425 where the testator, by a codicil, revoked the appointment of X as executor but then added that the will was to take effect 'as if her name was omitted from my will and as if she were dead'. X was named in the will as a principal beneficiary under referential trusts of the residuary estate and the court concluded that the testator did not intend to revoke the gift to X, merely the appointment. Evershed MR pointed out that the phrase has its origins in the early conveyancing precedents but, in the case of will drafting, its use should be confined to clauses revoking the appointment of executors.

Revocation by destruction

The other limb of s. 20, Wills Act 1837, makes provision for revocation of a testamentary instrument by destruction. There are two key elements which must be present in order for the testator to effect a valid revocation in this way: (1) the act of destruction; and (2) the intention (*animus revocandi*).

Section 20 refers to destruction by the words 'burning tearing or otherwise destroying the same'. In *Cheese* v *Lovejoy* (1877) 2 PD 251 the court construed the words 'or otherwise destroying the same' *eiusdem generis* with 'burning and tearing'. The Statute of Frauds had referred to 'cancelling' and in *Cheese* v *Lovejoy* the testator had written across the will 'cancelled' but the court refused to accept this as a valid act of destruction.

What does amount to destruction? Cutting someone out of the will — literally (!) as in *the Estate of Nunn* [1936] 1 All ER 555 where the testatrix decided to leave certain beneficiaries out of her will by cutting out the gifts and sticking the will together again. If the testatrix had stopped at that point, it would have been a partial revocation. However, sometime later the testatrix cut off her signature and those of the witnesses. This was considered to be an act of revocation of the whole will.

In *the Estate of Adams (dec'd)* [1990] 2 All ER 97 the testatrix had requested her will to be revoked. The solicitor sent her the original document. Five years later, following the death of the testatrix, the will was found among her papers scribbled over in several places by a blue-black ball-point pen. In addition, the signatures of the witnesses and the testatrix had been heavily scored over with a ball-point pen. The court held that there had been revocation and referred by analogy to s. 21 Wills Act 1837 on unattested alterations, asking the question 'were the names of the testatrix and witnesses apparent on the face of the instrument?'. As they were not, there had been a revocation of the whole will.

The act of destruction must be by the testator or someone in his presence and on his direction. This is to reduce the risk of fraud. So the action of the brother in burning the will in *Re Durance* (1872) would have been invalid. Revocation was effected because the letter, showing intention on the part of the testator to revoke the will, took effect as a testamentary direction.

The intention to revoke must be concurrent with the act of destruction. It follows that there is no revocation where the offices where the will is stored burn down, as in *Re Booth* [1926] P 118, or where, in a row between husband and wife, the wife tears up the husband's will, as in *Gill* v *Gill* [1909] P 157.

Let us return to eager Uriah whom we met at the beginning of this chapter. There is no revocation when he throws the will onto the fire for, although Uriah has burned the will, the act was not done in Tom's presence or on his direction. What does direction mean? In *Gill* v *Gill* the court said that direction means intention. When the wife tore up the will in the course of the row there was no revocation because there was no intention on the part of the testator at that time. Subsequently the husband took no steps to make another will and the evidence appears to suggest that he acquiesced in the act of destruction. However there was no valid revocation within s. 20, Wills Act 1837 because the act of destruction and the intention were not concurrent.

If the intention cannot be formed because of illness, or because the testator is suffering from the effects of drink or drugs there can be no revocation.

The doctrine of dependent relative revocation

A more difficult matter is in deciding whether conditional revocation applies; this is the so-called doctrine of dependent relative revocation. Where the testator purports to revoke a will on the basis that a new will is valid, or that the intestacy rules make the desired provision, but the new will is not valid, or the intestacy rules do not have the effect of making the expected provision, then the doctrine says that the old will remains effective.

At first the doctrine applied only where the beneficiaries under the old and the new wills were the same, but where there was e.g., some change in the amount of benefit to be received. *Onions* v *Tyrer* (1716) 2 Vern 741 is the first case cited on this topic although the reference to destruction of the earlier will is probably *obiter*. Here, the testator made a will containing certain devises. He later made a will altering some of the administrative provisions of the will but not altering the dispositive effect. According to the report he then destroyed the first will. The court held that the second will was invalid because it was not attested in the presence of the testator and he was held to have revoked his first will conditionally.

In *Re Middleton* (1864) 2 Sw & Tr 583 the testator made a will leaving a legacy to a niece. He then attempted to make a second will excluding the niece but the second will was invalid for want of proper attestation. The first will was then destroyed. The court held that the revocation of the first will was conditional upon the second will coming into force, so the first will remained operative.

The doctrine can now apply wherever the second will ceases to have effect, and for whatever reason. A good example of the application of the doctrine following a misunderstanding of the intestacy rules is *Re Southerden* [1925] P 177 where Pollock MR said

> . . . the true view may be that a revocation grounded on the assumption of fact which is false takes effect unless, as a matter of construction, the truth of the fact is the condition of the revocation, or, in other words, unless the revocation is contingent upon the fact being true.

In *Re Jones* [1976] 1 All ER 593 the Court of Appeal set out a series of questions in applying conditional revocation, emphasising that the mere fact that the testator intends to make a second will does not mean that revocation of the first will is conditional upon the second will being made. Here, there was evidence resulting from a conversation between the testatrix and her bank manager that the testatrix wanted to revoke residuary gifts to her nieces and make a new will in favour of her nephews. However, the destruction of the first will was not conditional upon another will taking effect. The testatrix had destroyed her first will, *animus revocandi*, and then turned her attention to the instructions for another will but died before this could be effected.

The doctrine has been considered in some detail in *Re Finnemore (dec'd)* [1992] 1 All ER 800. The testator (T) made a will leaving a house, contents and three-quarters of the residuary estate to X and the remaining quarter to Y and Z. Two years later, on 4 November 1986 the testator executed another will and executed a further will three weeks later. Both these wills of 1986 contained express revocation clauses. Will 1 of 1986 repeated the gift to X and gave the remaining quarter to two charities. Will 2 was identical except that the quarter share of residue was now divided between three charities. The two wills of 1986 were attested by X's husband thereby avoiding the gifts to X by virtue of s. 15, Wills Act 1837. The executor under the last will applied for directions as to whether, the gift to X having failed, the property should be held in trust for X on the basis that the express revocation clause was conditional or qualified, so that X would benefit under the first will; or whether the house, contents and three-quarters of the residue passed on intestacy. The court held that the express revocation clause could be given a distributive meaning. This enabled the court to say that such a clause could apply absolutely to some provisions, but only conditionally to others, thereby applying the doctrine of conditional revocation to save a gift struck down by s. 15. It was therefore appropriate to give the revocation clause in the testator's last will a distributive meaning in order to carry out the clear intention of the testator.

How does the court determine intention? By a construction of the last will and in the light of the surrounding circumstances which would include notice of the provisions of the two earlier wills. As an alternative finding, in *Re*

Finnemore (dec'd), the court held that the testator had mistakenly thought that the attestation of the last will by X's husband would not render the gift to X invalid and, as a result, the revocation of the first will was conditional upon the validity of the gift in the last will. This alternative ground would appear to be a wide application of the doctrine. The court added that the second ground did not subvert s. 15 since the gift to X was made in the first will which was unaffected by s. 15.

We must now return to Tom and his act of throwing the crumpled will onto his desk. Is this sufficient to constitute destruction within s. 20, Wills Act 1837? According to *Cheese v Lovejoy* (1871) it was not sufficient. Even if there was destruction of the will is the intention unqualified, or dependent upon the validity of a new will?

The decision in *Re Finnemore* would appear to reflect a wider application of the doctrine. Was the inclusion of the express revocation clause in the last will, compounded by the attestation by X's husband, a mistake of law or fact? Either way it does not appear to have made any difference in applying the doctrine of conditional revocation.

Although in *Re Finnemore* the court is giving effect to the intention of the testator who did not want the gift to X subverted by s. 15, the application of the doctrine does not always result in effect being given to the intention of the testator. By applying an earlier will on the strength of conditional revocation the court is ensuring that the testator does not die intestate as, for example, in *Re Middleton* (1864).

If the earlier will has been destroyed, but held to have been conditionally revoked, how do you prove the contents? Nowadays it is likely, where the will has been professionally prepared, that there would be a photocopy of the original completed will rather than a made-up draft. The leading case authority comes from the nineteenth century, and is the saga of the will of the former Lord Chancellor, Lord St. Leonards, cited as *Sugden v Lord St. Leonards* (1876) 1 PD 154. Proof of contents was given by St. Leonards' daughter who had acted as his secretarial assistant and could understand the phraseology. The evidence of the daughter was accepted despite her being a principal beneficiary for, in the words of the judgment, as the daughter of a former Lord Chancellor her veracity could not be impinged!

Revocation by subsequent marriage

The other limb to revocation is the automatic revocation of the will by the subsequent marriage of the testator (s. 18, Wills Act 1837). The rule applies in the case of a void or voidable marriage. Note the consequence in the case of a marriage voidable for want of capacity such as *Re Davey* (1980) (chapter 3), which conjures up scenes of the wealthy heiress marrying her lover and dying before being able to make a new will. To cater for any possible lacuna, since the making of a new will would not necessarily be the first thing on the minds of the bride and groom, s. 18 goes on to provide for a will to be made in expectation of marriage.

Section 18, Wills Act 1837 was revised by the Administration of Justice Act 1982, following the Law Reform Committee's 22nd Report which took account of the judgment of Megarry VC in *Re Coleman* [1975] 1 All ER 675, when the opportunity was taken to review the earlier case law and the interpretation of the now repealed s. 177, Law of Property Act 1925. A critical part of the interpretation by Megarry VC was that to apply s. 177, which concerned wills made in contemplation of marriage, the whole will had to be expressed to be in contemplation of marriage. This decision, which was perfectly correct, raised the possibility of the situation, e.g., where a widower with young children who is contemplating marrying again, makes a will in contemplation of marriage leaving property to his future wife and in addition makes provision in the will for his children. On the interpretation by Megarry VC, this will would be ineffective for the whole will is not made in contemplation of marriage, merely certain gifts. Watch in questions where a will is executed before 1 January 1983, for the will in that case will be governed by s. 177. Study the wording of the new section and see how the drafting deals with the problem posed by the decision in *Re Coleman*.

The revised s. 18 refers to wills made 'in expectation' of marriage. There have been no reported cases on the interpretation of 'expectation'. Cases so far have been concerned with the interpretation of 'contemplation' within the original s. 18. Megarry V-C in *Re Coleman* reviewed the cases on the meaning of contemplation. 'Expectation' suggests a wider interpretation although this remains to be tested.

The Administration of Justice Act 1982 added a new section, s. 18A, where, for deaths on or after 1 January 1983, a divorce subsequent to the will affects gifts to spouses. Section 18A provides that in the event of a divorce any gift to the spouse in the will, or appointment of the spouse as an executor, will lapse. The Court of Appeal in *Re Sinclair* [1985] 1 All ER 1066 considered the meaning of lapse and held that the section did not apply to trigger a gift over where the testator by his will gave all his property to his spouse, adding the common phrase 'if my wife shall pre-decease me . . .' then followed by a gift over to charity. The gift to the wife was revoked following the divorce. Did the charity take? As 'lapse' did not mean 'pre-decease' the charity did not take. The decision sent many lawyers hastily checking the wording of their clients' wills. Consider how you would word a gift over in the light of the decision in *Re Sinclair*.

Care needs to be taken in answering questions on ss. 18 and 18A, Administration of Justice Act 1982 on the operative dates. In the case of s. 18 the section applies to wills executed on or after 1 January 1983. In the case of s. 18A, the section operates for deaths occurring on or after 1

January 1983. Compare, for example, the effect of a will which leaves '£5,000 to my brother Henry and the remainder of my estate to my fiancée Olive', where the will is dated (a) 6 June 1980, and (b) 6 June 1985.

Alterations

Alterations to wills are governed by s. 21, Wills Act 1837. If the alteration to the will is executed and attested by the testator and the witnesses (initials suffice), there is no problem regarding the admission of the altered will to probate. One must make sure that the witnesses and testator sign, see *Re White (dec'd)* [1990] 3 All ER 1. If, however, there is no problem then there is no problem for you in the examination! Note the evidential presumption where the alteration is unattested.

If the altered amount is inadmissible for want of proof that it was made before or at the time of execution (the court would call for an affidavit from the witnesses or those instrumental in the preparation of the will), does the original gift take effect? If it is 'apparent on the face of the instrument' it will take effect. What does this mean? The court will not admit evidence based upon extraneous means such as infra-red photography or chemicals. Only the normal aids to eyesight may be used, unless the doctrine of conditional revocation can be invoked, as in *Re Itter* [1950] P 130 where the court admitted evidence based upon infra-red photography. The decision in *Townley* v *Watson* (1844) 3 Curt 761 shows that one cannot turn to a draft copy to see what was there before the alteration, because the wording of s. 21 does not indicate any admission of extrinsic evidence unless, again, one can invoke conditional revocation.

Republication

Section 34, Wills Act 1837 provides that where a will is re-executed or (more commonly) a codicil to the will is executed, the will is deemed to be read from the date of re-execution or the date of the codicil. Barton J in *Re Moore* [1907] 1 IR 315 said:

> . . . republication is not a rigid or technical rule, but a useful, flexible instrument for effectuating the testator's intentions by ascertaining them down to the latest date at which they have been expressed.

The section needs to be noted, for the effect of republication can appear in constructional questions where, for example, the question states 'would your answer differ if, three months before his death, the testator executed a codicil appointing an additional executor *but otherwise confirming his will?*'. Do not just answer 'yes', but consider the effect of republication by the confirmatory codicil.

Revival

Suppose Tom is intending to marry his beloved Olive. Tom executes a will leaving all his property to 'my beloved Olive'. Six months later Tom marries Olive. Three years later Tom is sorting out his papers, re-reads the will and places it in an envelope and writes on the envelope 'Olive is now my wife', signs below and his signature is attested by two friends. When Tom dies, leaving a substantial estate, he is survived by Olive and the children of the marriage. Olive asks if the will is admissible to probate. To advise Olive you have to consider not only s. 18, Wills Act 1837 but the provisions relating to revival in s. 22.

Where a will has been validly revoked, s. 22, Wills Act 1837 provides that the will can be revived, that is, brought back into effect, by re-execution or by a codicil which shows an intention to revive. Re-execution is straightforward. So long as the will is re-executed in accordance with s. 9, then the document will be admitted to probate as the last will. More difficult is the construction of codicils. Revival by codicil was considered in *Re Steele* (1868) LR 1 P&D 575 which illustrates that merely executing a codicil does not, in itself, effect revival. There must be a clear intention to revive, either by express words or some disposition or expression which is inconsistent with any other intention. So, merely taping a codicil to a will did not show sufficient intention in *Marsh* v *Marsh* (1860) 1 Sw & Tr 528. In *Re Dear* [1975] 2 NZLR 254, a case from New Zealand, the testatrix, by a will in 1950, expressly revoked her earlier will of 1942. In 1962 she executed a codicil referring to her will of 1942. However, the reference was unclear, merely creating an ambiguity, so the codicil did not revive the earlier will.

To effect revival one must keep within s. 22, so an earlier will cannot be revived by revocation of the revoking instrument; *Re Hodgkinson* [1893] P 339.

Revocation can occur by operation of law under s. 18. Could one revive a will previously unwittingly revoked on marriage? There is no direct authority on this point in English law. A Malaysian case interpreting similar legislation, *Re Wan Kee Cheong* (1975) suggests that one could.

Let us return to Olive and the children. What was the effect of the marriage on the will? It revoked the will under s. 18 for Tom did not describe Olive as his fiancée, thereby indicating expectation of marriage. At that stage, therefore, Tom would have died intestate. However, by writing the words on the envelope and signing in accordance with s. 9, Tom had executed a codicil to the will inside the envelope showing an intention to revive (see *In the Goods of Davis dec'd* [1952] P 279), therefore both the will and the envelope would be admitted to probate ensuring testate succession.

SIX

INTESTACY

Introduction

The study of the law of succession is founded upon two pillars; (1) testate succession, that is, devaluation according to the clear terms of a valid will, and (2) intestate succession, where there is no admissible will. Distribution may be upon a total intestacy, where the will fails completely or the deceased dies not having made a will, or on a partial intestacy where the distributive provisions of the will apply in part but fail to dispose of the entire estate. In any study of succession it is essential to be conversant with the rules of intestacy.

Before the great property reforms of 1925, real and personal estate devolved differently under the rules of intestate succession. Realty vested in the heir at law, whereas the personal estate of the intestate deceased rested in the personal representatives for the benefit of the next of kin. There were complicated rules to determine kinship and in certain cases the heir's right to the realty was subject to the rights of the surviving spouse. Rules laid down by the Statutes of Distributions of 1670 and 1685 set out the degrees of relationship.

Although the Statutes of Distributions dealt with distribution upon intestacy, the ecclesiastical courts, which retained jurisdiction in the law of wills until the middle of the nineteenth century, encouraged a belief that dying intestate was, at worst, tantamount to dying excommunicated and, at best, was a matter of shame to the family of the property.

In the early part of this century in the build up to the property reforms of 1925, a survey of the pattern of wills was carried out to determine the typical family pattern for the statutory distribution of property. Concern was expressed at the number of people who died intestate, either through reluctance or neglect to turn their attentions to the distribution of their property on death, or to the dangers inherent in not ensuring that their wills could pass muster as either formally valid or understandable. Such people were clearly deaf to the clarion call of Lord St. Leonards (yes, the one whose will was lost!) who declared:

. . . particularly warn against the use of printed forms which have misled many men. They are as dangerous as the country schoolmaster or the vestry clerk . . . to put off making your will until the hand of death is upon you evidences either cowardice or a shameful neglect of temporal concerns.

The rules of intestate distribution were re-cast as part of the property reforms of 1925. Since then the statutory rules have been the subject of committee scrutiny, most notably by the Morton Committee (1950) Cmd. 8310, which lead to the Intestates Estates Act of 1952, and a recent review by the Law Commission, No. 187 (1989). The circumstances leading to the Commission referral and the recommendations are considered at the end of this chapter.

Case study

Let us consider Ivan, who has to date not heeded the words of warning and doom uttered by Lord St. Leonards. Ivan is rather blasé about the thought of making his will. He has a carefree air, his mind is on the present rather than the future. Ivan is married to Jane. They have a daughter, Susan, and grandchildren, Ben and Eric, sons of their deceased son, Colin. In addition, Jane has a son, Andrew, from her previous marriage.

Ivan has built up a successful antiques business in premises adjacent to his house, 'The Villa', a large, Victorian property. All the members of the family live at 'The Villa', together with Ivan's father, Paul, and Jenny, Ivan's sister. 'The Villa', owned by Ivan, has a market value of £180,000. The antiques business is worth £280,000 including stock. In addition Ivan has investments of £80,000, an estate car worth £10,000 and a coin collection worth £20,000. Ivan inherited the coin collection from his grandfather and, for the past ten years, he has deposited the collection with his bank for safe keeping. In addition, there is furniture and personal items worth £14,000.

Two years ago, Ivan gave Susan £10,000 to assist her in a retail clothes business she owns in association with her friend, Declan, and Ivan gave Ben £12,000 towards securing provision to assist Ben's first steps in practice at the Bar.

Ivan is a robust, outspoken character, successful in business. He has, to date, been dismissive of advice from his solicitor, Frank, that he should make a will. His response to Frank is always the same: 'I made one once when I did my National Service, but tore it up years ago. The thought of it gave me the creeps'.

Keep in mind Ivan, his family and assets as we consider intestate distribution. We can then return to Ivan and assist Frank in explaining to Ivan the consequences of his lack of testamentary action.

Look Will lad, give 'em a ring and find out what all the fuss is about

Intestate distribution — the trust for sale

The law relating to intestate distribution is largely contained in statutory codes. Section 33, Administration of Estates Act 1925, imposes a trust for sale and, after the payment of funeral, testamentary and administration expenses, debts and other liabilities (and any pecuniary legacies in the case of a partial intestacy), the personal representatives hold the residue for distribution in accordance with the order of entitlement under s. 46. The statutory order of entitlement must be studied in detail.

In the case of a partial intestacy, the trust for sale has a limited application. *Re McKee* [1931] 2 Ch 145, shows that where the deceased has, by will, disposed of a limited interest in property, in this case a life interest to his wife, the statutory trust did not apply to the residue undisposed of by the will. Therefore a sale of assets was not obligatory. The reason was that the will had already imposed an express trust for sale. In this case the partial intestacy was caused by a lapsed gift of residue. In *Re Bowen-Buscarlet's Will Trusts* [1971] 3 All ER 636 there was no gift of residue after the will had left a life interest to the widow. Again, the statutory trust had no application, thereby enabling the widow to claim the statutory legacy under the ensuing partial intestacy.

The approach to intestate distribution

A sound approach to the problem that can arise where the intestacy rules apply, either wholly or in part, is to break the problem into two columns. In one column list all those persons who are potentially entitled to benefit in accordance with the statutory order. Do not simply list those whom you know can benefit, but include all those who survive the intestate in their correct order of entitlement. The advantage of this full list is that it will give you the order of entitlement to a grant to the estate of the intestate deceased (with the addition at the end of the Crown and any creditors) in accordance with Rule 22, Non-Contentious Probate Rules 1987. In column two are listed the assets of the deceased passing on the intestacy and their value. When you study the statutory order you see the cut-off points depending upon who survives the intestate.

If we keep in mind the frustrating task Frank has in trying to persuade Ivan to make a new will, let us consider the entitlement to assets in the event of Ivan dying intestate.

Suppose we list all those entitled according to the statutory order. This would be: Jane, Susan, Ben and Eric, then Paul followed by Jenny. Jane qualifies to benefit as she is the lawful spouse of a valid, subsisting marriage. The order continues (in part) issue, parents, brothers and sisters of the whole blood. What does this tell us about the order? Apart from Jane, whose entitlement is based upon marriage, the remaining entitlement follows the blood line of the intestate deceased. Notice the next category, i.e., issue, does not say 'children', a common error made in the examination hall. 'Issue' here will mean Susan, Ben and Eric. Notice that Andrew is not included for he is not issue of Ivan. He may have a close relationship with his step-father, but step-children are not included in the statutory order on intestacy. Andrew may be entitled under the family provision legislation as a 'child of the family' or as a dependant. An alternative approach would be a possible claim for proprietary estoppel on the authority of *Re Basham dec'd* [1987] 1 All ER 405.

Ben and Eric will be included for they step into the share which their deceased father, Colin, would have taken if he had survived Ivan. Distribution is upon a *per stirpial* basis, so that the share to the issue would be divided two ways, one to a fund for Susan, the other to the 'Colin fund'. Ben and Eric would then take one half each of Colin's share. The fact that Jane and the issue survive would preclude Paul and Ivan's sister, Jenny, from any benefit. However, they would be entitled to apply for the administration of the estate if Jane and the issue were unwilling or incapable of so doing.

Once it is decided who is entitled to benefit, one can turn to column two and assess the entitlement. Jane, as surviving spouse, would be entitled to the personal chattels absolutely; the fixed net sum known as the statutory legacy and a life interest in half of the remainder of the estate. Here we are into a favourite area for the examination, i.e., the rights of the surviving spouse on intestacy.

Personal chattels

Personal chattels are defined by the rather dated s. 55(1)(x) of the Administration of Estates Act 1925. The section is unsatisfactory in that there are specific items listed, followed by the general words 'articles of household and personal use'. The reference to the specific items is out of date, e.g., '. . . carriages, horses, stable furniture . . . plated articles, linen, china, glass . . .' and so on. The section specifically excludes articles used for business purposes, money and securities. Litigation over particular items in the case law has considered inclusion by analogy with the listed items, or by reference to the general words 'articles of household or personal use or ornament'. So, for example, in *Re Reynolds Will Trusts* [1966] 1 WLR 19 the court said that a stamp album was not a book within the specific reference to books but that the album was an article of personal use, and therefore came within the definition.

Why the litigation? There are two reasons; (1) items can acquire a high monetary value, and (2) personal chattels pass to the spouse absolutely. The case law on the interpretation of the section is not confined to intestacy situations. It is a relatively common provision in wills for the testator to bequeath 'all my personal chattels, as defined by s. 55(1)(x) . . .'. In *Re Whitby* [1944] Ch 210, cut but unmounted diamonds were held to come within the section under the specific reference to jewellery, the court citing the Oxford English Dictionary meaning as '. . . jewellers' work, gems or ornaments made or sold by jewellers'.

An interesting and authoritative judgment on the construction of s. 55(1)(x) is by the Court of Appeal in *Re Crispin's Will Trusts* [1975] 1 Ch 245. The testator had inherited a large collection of clocks and watches, a collection which he had helped to build up. Following his inheritance the testator never added to the collection which was kept in locked rooms and chests, although essential repairs were carried out and, from time to time (no pun intended!) the testator wore one of the watches. In a bequest to his sister, did the collection fall within the statutory definition where the market value of the collection at the date of death accounted for over sixty per cent of the total value of the estate?

At first instance, the Vice-Chancellor thought it improbable that the testator intended to make over a high value gift to his sister. However, the Court of Appeal rejected this line. In their view the issue was: 'did the items come within the definition?': their value was immaterial. The court held that the clocks were furniture and the watches items of personal use. The court rejected a distinction between buying such a collection and inheriting, thereby casting doubt upon the dictum of (appropriately) Stamp J in *Re Reynolds* (1966) when he appeared to reject the idea of a stamp collection as an item of personal use if it had been purchased by the deceased.

One can anticipate difficulties in Ivan's estate for we are told that he is an antiques dealer. In *Re Ogilby* [1942] Ch 288 the court had to consider whether cattle on a farm belonging to the intestate which was not worked for a profit, came within the reference to domestic animals. 'No' said the court, for although the farm was not worked at a profit, it was still a business.

The statutory legacy

The surviving spouse is entitled to a fixed net sum which carries interest at 6 per cent per annum. The amount, which can be altered by statutory instrument, rose steeply through the 1970s and 1980s in view of inflation, particularly in relation to land values. The main problem giving rise to pressure on the amount of the statutory legacy is the rise in property values which has created an imbalance in the distribution to the spouse on any intestacy where the spouse wishes to secure continuing occupation of the former matrimonial home. The statutory legacy is currently set at £75,000 if the intestate is survived by issue, and £125,000 where there are no surviving issue.

Rights to the matrimonial home

Suppose the spouse wishes to remain in the former matrimonial home following the death of the intestate. First, the title to the home must be considered. Is the property in the joint names as joint tenants or tenants in common? If the property is in the sole name of the intestate deceased, can the surviving spouse establish a claim under an implied or resulting trust under the principles laid down in *Pettit* v *Pettit* [1970] AC 777 or *Gissing* v *Gissing* [1971] AC 886? Before you turn to look with dismay at the syllabus, let me tell you that you will not face detailed questions based on these cases but you need to be aware of them in this important, practical area of rights to the matrimonial home.

Where the matrimonial home is in the joint names, consider whether the spouses hold as joint tenants or tenants in common. If the property is held as joint tenant, then the title and value of the half share of the deceased will pass automatically to the survivor by virtue of the *ius accrescendi* and will not count towards any entitlement which the surviving spouse may have on the intestacy.

Where the title is in the sole name of the intestate deceased and rights in trust cannot be established, the surviving spouse has the right to require the personal representatives to appropriate the matrimonial home in satisfaction against absolute entitlement on the intestacy. The surviving spouse could, therefore, use a part or, if necessary, the whole of the statutory legacy in exercising her right of appropriation. The value of the home may exceed the value of the statutory legacy. In *Re Phelps Dec'd* [1979] 3 All ER 373 the court held that the spouse could still exercise the appropriation of the home on payment of the difference between the statutory legacy and the market value.

In order to exercise the right of appropriation, the surviving spouse must have been resident in the home at the time of death. What about the situation where the deceased owned two homes? Residence is an umbrella concept, therefore if the surviving spouse demonstrates that, as a couple, they use both homes, the survivor can elect on which home to serve notice of appropriation. The decision needs to be taken quickly, particularly in a rising property market. Although the spouse has twelve months from the date of death the value is taken at the date of appropriation.

The serving of notice of appropriation on the personal representatives does not mean that the spouse is automatically entitled to the home, given that the spouse has the requisite funds. Note the grounds upon which the personal representatives may refuse to transfer title. The principle underlying a number of the statutory reasons for refusal is to prevent a diminution in the value of the estate. The personal representatives owe a duty to the beneficiaries as a whole to preserve the value of estate assets.

The life interest

Where issue survive the intestate deceased, the surviving spouse is entitled to a life interest in one half of the remainder of the estate. The spouse may elect to capitalise the life interest in accordance with s. 47A (3A) and (3B), Administration of Estates Act, 1925 and with the Intestate Succession (Interest and Capitalisation) Order 1977, SI 1977 No. 1491. It is not necessary to have a detailed knowledge of the calculation. The principle underlying the calculation is to create a lump sum which could be used to purchase an annuity for that particular person, that is a person that age and sex, as the calculation is based upon life expectancy.

Why capitalise? The spouse may find an actuarial lump sum is more useful, giving the spouse greater flexibility in immediate plans rather than drawing an income for the rest of life. The fund supporting the life interest may not be large, therefore capitalisation may be more beneficial rather than incurring regular administration expenses in respect of the life interest.

The issue

Where the intestate dies survived by spouse and issue, no one else may claim under the intestacy distribution. Who are the issue? What is their entitlement? Remember one is considering issue of the intestate deceased and not children of both spouses. Hence, in advising Ivan, Frank would point out that stepson Andrew, however close he may be in affection to Ivan, would not be entitled under the intestacy. The issue entitled, should Ivan die intestate, would be Susan, Ben and Eric. They take their half share of the residue on the statutory trusts under s. 47, Administration of Estates Act 1925 that is, their interests are contingent on their attaining the age of eighteen or earlier marriage.

In analysing questions upon intestate distribution where issue are included, one should look to three key areas:

(a)   the statutory trusts;
(b)   the *per stirpial* distribution; and
(c)   evidence of any *inter vires* advances under s. 47(1)(iii) which must be brought into account against the individual shares on the intestacy.

Hotchpot — the first taste

There are two 'hotchpot' provisions to consider in relation to intestacy; advances under s. 47(1)(iii) and the more complicated rules on accounting for benefits under the will in s. 49(1)(aa) to which we will return later.

Before you reach for receipe books, 'hotchpot' does not relate to a course in home economics. The hotchpot provisions are based upon the principle of equality, that is, in the absence of any contrary intention, the intestate deceased intended that those entitled to share in the estate assets should be treated equally. If some beneficiaries have already received substantial benefits, they should bring these into account against further benefits received either under the will or upon the intestacy.

Section 47(1)(iii) requires any 'advance' made for the benefit of a child of the intestate to be brought into account against the share that child would receive on the intestacy. Two words stand out here: 'advance' and 'child'. An advance is some substantial provision whose purpose is to set the person up in life, that is, more than a mere gift *inter vivos*. Provision of capital on the marriage of the child is also an advance. The donor may indicate that the advance should not be brought into account so long as that contrary intention is clearly expressed. The burden of proving a contrary intention rests with the recipient child. The test is positive, i.e., did the donor intend to prefer that child in terms of the amount and time of receipt? On the meaning of advance read *Taylor* v *Taylor* [1875] LR 20 Eq 155; *Re Hayward* [1957] Ch

528 and *Hardy* v *Shaw* [1976] Ch 82. The last case considered the question of the contrary intention, and it is also a good example of filial falling out!

Let us return to Frank and his task of persuading Ivan to make a will. Frank decides to outline how the estate would be distributed if Ivan died intestate. The distribution ignores any claims which may be made against the estate under the family provision legislation.

Jane, as surviving spouse, would be entitled to the personal chattels applying in s. 55(1)(x). There could be problems here, given Ivan's occupation, for one would have to decide which items were personal chattels and which formed part of the business stock. In addition, there is specific mention of the coin collection which, provided it is not part of the business assets, would pass to Jane absolutely on the authority of *Re Crispin's Will Trusts* (1975).

Jane is entitled to a statutory legacy of £75,000 and a life interest in half of the remainder of the estate. Jane would have to consider, as soon as possible, whether she would want to serve notice of appropriation in respect of 'The Villa'. Could she afford to appropriate? Would she consider a capitalisation of the life interest? The other half of the residue would be divided two ways, i.e., the 'Susan fund' and the 'Colin fund', with Ben and Eric taking a half each of the Colin fund. The ages of the issue are not given but their respective ages would have to be borne in mind in applying the statutory trusts.

The £10,000 given to Susan would appear to be an advance, applying *Taylor* v *Taylor* (1875). Therefore, Susan will have to bring this into account against her share on the intestacy. If the gift to Susan is an advance so is, you will say, the £12,000 given to Ben to assist him in his career. Yes, it is an advance but Ben does not have to account on the intestacy because Ben is a grandchild and not a child. How does Susan account? Suppose the value of one half of the residuary estate is £220,000. The value of the advance would be added, giving a total of £230,000. The fund would then be divided as to £115,000 to Susan and £115,000 to the Colin Fund. The £10,000 would then be deducted from the Susan fund reducing her share to £105,000 and leaving the Colin fund at £115,000.

'Issue'

In considering the meaning of issue, one has to consider the entitlement of illegitimate, adopted and legitimated children and the effect of annulment and divorce. The Administration of Estates Act 1925 originally applied to legitimate children of the intestate deceased and their issue. There have been a number of statutory changes since 1925, culminating in the Family Law Reform Act 1987. You are unlikely to face a question devoted to contrasting the rights of illegitimate children as against legitimate children.

However, individual points do appear and the changes in relation to child status and rights need to be studied. Note the effect of the marriage contract, for example, in the case of a voidable marriage dissolved after 31 July 1971. The marriage is annulled from the date of the decree and any children born before annulment will be legitimate. A void marriage on the other hand is no marriage but a child born of the union can be regarded as legitimate if, at the time of the conception, both parties reasonably believed that they were validly married. This will only apply where the parties have gone through a ceremony of marriage and not to children born before such a ceremony (*Re Spence* [1990] 2 All ER 827).

Where parents of a child illegitimate at birth subsequently validly marry each other, the child will be legitimated from the date of the marriage; s. 5(4), Legitimacy Act 1976. Therefore, the child will be able to share on the parents' intestacy in the same way as brothers and sisters born legitimately. In the case of the death of an intestate parent on or after 1 January 1970, the Family Law Reform Act 1969 puts the illegitimate child on an equal footing with legitimate brothers and sisters as regards sharing in the estate of the intestate parent. However, such a child could not share on the intestacy of any other relative. These restrictions have been removed for deaths intestate after 4 April 1988 by the Family Law Reform Act 1987. The statute effectively removes the distinction between legitimate or illegitimate for the purposes of distribution. The adopted child assumes all rights in the estate of the adopting parents and has all rights of succession to the estate of the natural parents.

Remaining entitlement

The remainder of the list of those entitled on an intestate distribution must be known. A point to keep in mind in regard to the order of distribution in general is the effect of a disclaimer of an interest by a person entitled under the order. Where a person who is entitled higher in the order disclaims, this will accelerate the interests of their beneficiaries in the next category unless the interest is contingent. If the interest is contingent, acceleration will not occur, see *Re Scott (dec'd)* [1975] 2 All ER 1033. A question which remains unanswered is, if a sole child disclaims, does that benefit that child's issue, that is, the grandchildren of the intestate, or does the disclaimer benefit the next category, i.e., parents of the intestate?

Partial intestacy

We must sympathise with Frank who has patiently explained what would happen if Ivan failed to make a will. Ivan himself, on the other hand, is recovering from trying to understand the principle of hotchpot which he has imagined is some kind of preparation Frank would cook up if Ivan does not pay Frank's fees! Frank now takes a deep breath to answer Ivan's next query. What would happen if a will is made but for some reason the will fails to dispose of the entire estate? Sympathies go out to Frank as he sets out to explain how a partial intestacy could arise and the complicated hotchpot provisions which could follow.

A partial intestacy will result where a share of the residue under the will fails to take effect. For example, the residuary share could lapse by the beneficiary named failing to survive the testator or by application of s. 15, Wills Act 1837. Partial intestacy is governed by s. 49, Administration of Estates Act 1925 and involves applying the order of intestate distribution to those who survive the deceased. This in itself is relatively straightforward. The questions involving partial intestacy usually turn upon the accounting provisions where a beneficiary receives benefits under the will and is entitled, at the same time, to share in the partial intestacy.

Suppose Simon by his will leaves a legacy of £50,000 to his wife, Ann (she has already been well provided for during his life) and the remainder of the estate after the payment of funeral, testamentary and administration expenses, debts and other liabilities, to his children, Charlie and Dan in equal shares absolutely. Dan dies before Simon without issue. There is, therefore, a partial intestacy as to half of the residuary estate. Ann and Charlie as surviving spouse and issue are entitled to share in the partial intestacy but they must account under s. 49(1), Administration of Estates Act 1925 for the benefits received under the will. By s. 49(1)(aa), Ann must set the legacy of £50,000 against her entitlement to the statutory legacy on the intestacy, thereby reducing the share of the statutory legacy to £25,000. Ann is then entitled to a life interest in one half of the remaining share on the intestacy; the other half devolves to Charlie on the statutory trusts.

The hotchpot rules under s. 49 are complex and can create anomalies. Suppose Simon had not given Ann a legacy but a life interest in half of the residue and the other half had been left to Charlie and Dan. Suppose Dan has survived Simon. There will still be a partial intestacy on the death of Simon because there is no gift over of one half of the residue after the life interest to Ann. Ann would have to bring into account the capital value of her life interest against her share on the partial intestacy. This will reduce or even eliminate the statutory legacy to Ann. Compare the situation if Simon had died totally intestate when Ann would be entitled to the statutory legacy and the life interest.

'I told you I should not make a will' shouts Ivan triumphantly. Frank merely groans.

More problematic in the partial intestacy is the accountability of the issue. Section 49(1)(a) provides:

the requirements of s. 47 (of this Act) as to bringing property into account shall apply to any beneficial interests acquired by any issue of the deceased under the will of the deceased; but not to beneficial interests so acquired by any other persons.

The section is poorly drafted and problems as to the extent of accountability have arisen from the mis-match between the reference to 'children' in s. 47(1)(iii) and 'issue' in s. 49(1)(a). Children must bring into account advances, that is, substantial benefits received from the deceased during his lifetime. This is the same as upon a total intestacy.

Section 49(1)(a) provides that children and remoter issue must bring into account beneficial interests acquired under the operative provisions of the will. Problems on the construction of s. 49(1)(a) centre on the situation where successive interests are left by will to the children and remoter issue. The courts have adopted two forms of construction of s. 49(1)(a), a stirpial construction and a distributive construction. The facts and judgments in *Re Young's Will Trusts* [1950] 2 All ER 1040, *Re Morton* [1956] 3 All ER 259 and *Re Grover's Will Trusts* [1970] 1 All ER 1185 need to be studied carefully.

The question before the court in each case concerned the extent of the interest under the will which had to be brought into account against the share on the partial intestacy. In *Re Young*, Harman J construed 'issue' to mean 'children or remoter issue'. This resulted in treating the life interest given to a son with remainder to the son's children as one gift, thereby requiring the son to account for the full capital value of the fund against his share of the partial intestacy. *Re Young* has been followed in *Re Morton* and *Re Grover's Will Trusts*. In *Re Grover*, Pennycuick J suggested a distributive construction as an alternative solution. The effect of adopting this line of construction would mean that each beneficiary would bring into account merely the value of their interest alone. However, in *Re Grover*, Pennycuick J applied the stirpial construction. The issue here is the fact that when separate interests exist in the same property, the aggregate value of those interests will only rarely be equivalent to the value of the property itself. Pennycuick J decided that *Re Young* and *Re Morton* would not be in conflict. In *Re Young* the interests of the child and the child's children amounted to the entire interest in the fund, therefore it was natural to bring the capital into account as the sum of the beneficial interests in the fund. In *Re Morton* there were no other beneficial interests in the fund so that method could not be adopted. The alternative, therefore, was to value severally the beneficial interests.

Ivan has begun to appreciate that dying intestate is not such a good idea and cheers Frank with the news that he will shortly give instructions for the preparation of a will. The proposals contained in the next section will also

cheer those who have grappled with the complexities and inter-action of
s. 47(1)(iii) and s. 49(1)(a).

The reform of intestate distribution

The Law Commission has reviewed the law relating to intestate distribution
and the resulting report, No. 187 (1989) needs to be studied. There was a
widely held recognition that the present law was in need of reform.

Background

There have been considerable changes in society since the review by the
Morton Committee in 1950. The 1960s saw an expansion in home
ownership, a trend which has continued until the present time. Allied to the
increase in home ownership is the move towards joint ownership of property
either between spouses or co-habitees. In addition there has been a
recognition that, increasingly, private property passes irrespective of the
terms of a will or the rules of intestacy; e.g., nominated pension rights and
declarations of trusts in respect of life policies. However, it is the change in
the pattern of home ownership, coupled with the increase in the value of the
matrimonial home, which draws into focus the need for reform. Until the
end of the 1980s there had been a gradual increase in private property values
with occasional 'spurts' such as in the early and late 1970s and, in particular,
in 1986-1988. The rapid rise in values in the late 1980s heightened the debate
about the North-South divide within the United Kingdom, a debate which
includes as a key issue the discrepancy in property values between the
regions. The rapid increase in house prices, particularly in the south of
England, increased the problems attached to the acquisition of the
matrimonial home by the surviving spouse on intestacy and highlighted the
inadequacy of the fixed net sum. One simple solution would have been to
increase greatly the amounts in the case of the statutory legacy. However,
the view prevailed that a more thorough review of intestate distribution was
required, particularly in relation to the rights of the spouse.

Defects in the present law

The Law Commission identified the following defects in the present law.

(1)   Inadequate provisions for the surviving spouse, in particular, in
relation to the statutory legacy which is often inadequate to meet a wish to
remain in the matrimonial home. The present rules are arbitrary and often
appear unfair since they do not draw any distinction as to how the home is
owned, for example, as a joint tenancy, tenancy in common, or rented (with

or without statutory rights of tenure or the right to buy the freehold). Disparities arise when, from time to time, the statutory legacy has to be raised to take account of inflation.

(2)   The expectations of other close relatives such as children will depend not upon how well the surviving parent is provided for, but upon the nature and tenure of the deceased parent's assets.

(3)   In certain cases the rules are complex and expensive to administer (Ivan nods vigorously when he reads this point).

The Law Commission rejected a straightforward major increase in the statutory legacy. Also the Commission rejected splitting distribution so that the matrimonial home would pass to the spouse plus the statutory legacy. Neither solution would, in the opinion of the Commission, solve the disparities and problems inherent in inflation.

Recommendations for future reform

The recommendations of the Law Commission are:

(1)   On intestacy the surviving spouse should receive the whole of the estate, subject to the provision of survivorship for fourteen days. This *simpliciter* solution removes the problems surrounding acquisition of the matrimonial home; the effect of inflation on the statutory legacy. There would be no further need for the power of appropriation, nor for the statutory trusts which are considered cumbersome and complex. Further there would be no longer a need for the dated definition of personal chattels.

(2)   A repeal of the hotchpot provisions.

(3)   No change is proposed to the order of distribution where there is no surviving spouse nor issue surviving the intestate deceased.

(4)   No change to the rule on *bona vacantia*. An alternative of disposition of the estate of an intestate with no surviving blood relations to charity was rejected.

Criticism

The Law Commission did consider criticism of its proposals. Constantly the review which led to the recommendations and the criticism of these recommendations is going to be an interesting topic for the examination room; in particular, the key recommendation that all the property of the intestate deceased passes to the surviving spouse. Where does this leave the children of the intestate? The Commission took the view that young children living with the surviving parent would be provided for by that parent. The children would have rights under the Children Act 1989 and, in the case of step-children, a possible claim as a 'child of the family' within the Inheritance Act 1975 (see chapter 7). The Commission rejected the criticism that the recommendation does not make for efficient tax planning by saying that the function of the intestacy rules is not to minimise tax liability. Further, the Law Commission rejected drawing distinctions between separate spouses and those living together or surviving spouses from second or subsequent marriages (in the latter case giving the issue of former marriages statutory rights), saying that the merits of each case need to be considered.

A suggestion that the issue of former marriages should be included in the statutory distribution was rejected as this could affect adequate provision for the surviving spouse. The prevailing view was that only discretionary provision would be able to take account of the relative merits of the spouse and issue. Here, the alternatives of making a will, the ordinary law of child maintenance and the family provision legislation are better adopted to take account of merit.

There is no indication as to when the recommendations, which include draft legislation, will proceed to become law. The pressure on parliamentary time and the political nature of such legislation often means that years elapse before major statutory changes are made. So, it would appear to be some way in the future before Frank can say to Ivan, 'well, you see, distribution is quite simple really'.

Question

'The definition of personal chattels in s. 55(1)(x) of the Administration of Estates Act 1925 is outmoded and should be repealed.' Discuss.

Comment

This question is asking you to consider the present definition and then attempt a critique. It is not necessary to write out the sub-section verbatim. Knowledge of the sub-section will be demonstrated by the analysis backed by the authority of cases demonstrating how the sub-section has been interpreted.

Section 55(1)(x) of the Administration of Estates Act 1925 defines 'personal chattels' by enumerating specific items such as horses, stables, furniture and refers to 'articles of household or personal use'. Cases have sought to include disputed items within the specific chattels referred to in the definition. In *Re Hutchinson* [1955] Ch 255, for example, the reference to 'horses' was held to include racehorses owned by the deceased at death for the purpose of recreation as opposed to business use. The court said there was nothing in the section to suggest the specific reference to 'horses' should be confined to domestic animals.

In *Re Reynolds Will Trusts* [1965] 3 All ER 686 there was argument to the effect that a stamp album was a 'book' within the section. Stamp J rejected this argument but held that the item came within the general words that a stamp album was intrinsically an article of personal use and enjoyment. Evidence was given that the album was maintained by the deceased as a main hobby, thereby supporting the interpretation based upon personal use. This interpretation was applied in *Re Collin's Settlement Trusts* [1971] 1 All ER 283, another case involving a stamp collection. Here the collection was worth approximately £15,000 out of a total net estate of £25,000.

Articles of business use are specifically excluded by the section. Where the object is used partly for business and partly for pleasure one would look for evidence of the main purpose of the usage. In *Re MacCulloch's Estate* [1981] NSR (2d) 666 (Nova Scotia) the testator bequeathed to his wife 'all articles of personal, domestic or household use or ornament'. The disputed chattel was a motor yacht owned by the deceased and moored at a country waterside property. The deceased and his wife used the property together with the yacht from time to time; the remainder of the time the property together with the yacht were let. Here, in considering the main purpose, the court concluded that the yacht was used principally for commercial purposes.

In *Re Ogilby* [1942] Ch 288 a herd of cattle owned by the intestate did not come within the definition as they were used for farming purposes. An argument based upon evidence that the farm operated at a loss and therefore was not a commercial venture, was rejected.

The interpretation of the words of the section have in a number of cases come before the court where the deceased has died testate but has bequeathed chattels by using the words of the sub-section, as in *Re Collin's Will Trusts* and *Re MacCulloch's Estate* as well as where there is a bequest in a will by direct reference to s. 55(1)(x) such as *Re Crispin's Will Trusts* [1974] 3 All ER 772.

In *Re Crispin* the court had to consider whether the bequest included a collection of clocks and watches, the 'Todhunter collection', bequeathed to the testator by one Todhunter. The testator maintained the collection in good working order but never added to it during his life. The collection was valued at his death at £51,000 out of a total gross estate of £83,000. The Vice-Chancellor held the collection did not come within the definition in s. 55. The case raised the question of a possible half-way house between personal use and business use, that is, objects held for investment, given that the collection had been inherited and, though kept intact, had never been increased.

The Court of Appeal took the view that the Vice-Chancellor was perhaps influenced by the disproportionate value of the collection in relation to the total value of the estate. The court held that the clocks came within the reference to 'furniture' within the section. The watches in the collection were held to be, by their very nature, objects of personal use. The case is in accord with the wider approach adopted in cases such as *Re Reynolds* and *Re Collin's Will Trusts*. In *Collins* the stamp collection accounted for a large proportion of the value of the estate at death.

Section 55(1)(x) has been criticised. The opening words '. . . carriages, horses, stables furniture and effects . . .' is dated. Commentators take the view that the section, despite its age, does work. However the Law Commission in their report on intestacy (Law Com. 1987) recommends that where the intestate is survived by his or her spouse the surviving spouse should take the entire estate. This would obviate the need for interpretation in the case of intestate estates. Whether this proposal is adopted or, if it was, whether the section would still remain on the statute book so that reference can be made in wills (as in *Re Crispin*), remains to be seen.

SEVEN

FAMILY PROVISION

Introduction

You have made it! Examinations are successfully behind you. You are qualified and sitting behind your mahogany desk reading the will of a long standing client of the firm, the late Tom Cartwright. Before you are seated the immediate members of the family. After pointing out the appointment of your firm as executors to the estate you reach the part they have been waiting for, the distribution of the estate. 'To my dear wife, Ruby, my house "The Gables" its contents and investments to the value of £500,000.' (Murmurs of 'what a wonderful husband'.) 'To my daughter, Kate, investments to the value of £300,000.' (Murmurs of 'what a wonderful father, always so generous'.) 'To my brother-in-law, Henry, who said I would never remember him in my will, hello Henry'.

The good news is that I have made a will. The bad news is that you're not in it.

This chapter is concerned with what action Henry could take, if any, and the rights of Ruby and Kate if Tom had not been so generous.

The will, and consequent actions

English law, unlike some continental systems, has not provided for automatic set portions of an estate of a deceased to pass to the close relatives. Instead it has preserved freedom of disposition but provided a form of restraint in giving certain people rights to apply to the court for provision from the estate where they consider they have not received their just deserts. Complete freedom over testamentary dispositions under English law only applied in the period from 1926 until 1938. Prior to 1926 real property passed to the heir at law and in 1938 the first family provision legislation was passed giving a right to apply to a limited class of dependants. You will have studied how the range of potential applicants, and the powers of the court to make orders for provision, were greatly extended by the Inheritance (Provision for Family and Dependants) Act 1975. The effect of the Act has been to preserve freedom of disposition but also to give the courts wide discretionary powers over the disposition of estates.

The 1975 Act exerts such an influence over the beneficial distribution that a thorough knowledge of the legislation is fundamental. Cases tend to turn on their particular facts and the questions tend to be in the form of problems. In order to 'set the scene' the examination questions can be long. Examples of the type of question are given later in this chapter.

The initial steps

It is no good for Henry simply to weep into his drink. What steps should Henry, as the thwarted beneficiary, consider? First of all the will and the circumstances surrounding its execution should be examined. Did the testator have the requisite testamentary intention? Was this freely formed? Are there any defects in the formal requirements of execution? Although these are initial steps which the practitioner looks for, you will appreciate that two major topics have been referred to, namely capacity and formal validity. Both these topics are important in practice and favourite examination topics. The result is that in a family provision question, the question itself may indicate that you should exclude any reference to, say, capacity. In such a case, and without any additional factual information, you can assume the will is correctly executed. Do not go on at length about formal validity where the facts do not call for this, simply because you want to demonstrate to the examiner that you have revised that particular topic; this approach does not impress!

Inheritance (Provision for Family and Dependants) Act 1975

What are we left with after these initial considerations? If there is no
evidence to challenge the validity of the will, or the question specifically asks
us to ignore that point, then we resort to the 1975 Act. Remember to reduce
the key issue to clearly expressed, concise points. This also aids your recall of
the topic. In order to succeed under the 1975 Act the applicant must prove
three things: (i) that the deceased died domiciled in England or Wales; (ii)
that he or she has the *locus standi* to apply to the court and (iii) that the will
and/or intestacy has failed to make reasonable provision for the applicant.

Domicile is a minimal point for our purposes. Detailed questions on the
meaning of domicile are going to appear on a paper on the conflict of laws
not succession. In any event the problem has diminished in the law of
succession since a married woman can now acquire a domicile of her choice,
whereas prior to 1973 she was stuck with the domicile of her husband.

Note, however, that the right to apply for reasonable provision is a
personal one and does not pass to the applicant's personal representatives.
This point has been a popular one of late in examinations. For example, you
are asked to advise, among others, the widow of the deceased as to her
chances of success under the 1975 Act. However, the question goes on to
inform you that the widow died some three months after the deceased
husband. This point is based upon the decision in *Whytte* v *Ticehurst* (1986)
Fam 64 where the court ruled that the right to apply died with the applicant.
Note, though, that the fact of the death can adjust the perceptions of benefit
of other potential claimants to the estate.

Locus standi

So far as *locus standi* is concerned, the categories of applicant set out in
s. 1(1)(a)-(e) must be known. For the sake of clarity, in examining the
different categories, this work spells out again who can apply under the
different paragraphs. The student should, however, know immediately if a
particular paragraph is mentioned, for example, (c) or (e), which persons
within the question could claim under those paragraphs.

Paragraph (a) — husband or wife of the deceased — is reasonably
straightforward. A problem here is the situation where, e.g., the wife has re-
married and application is being made by her in the estate of the deceased,
second husband. The court will need to be satisfied, on the available
evidence, that the first husband was dead at the time of the second marriage.
Here one has to consider the material on presumption of death. For
example, what contact has there been with the first husband's family? Has
anything been heard of him (not through a seance!)? Have there been any
claims on insurance policies?

Watch for the situation where the spouses are judicially separated: they are still husband and wife but, under s. 15(1) the question of provision may have been dealt with in the order at the time of the separation. This does not necessarily prevent an application as one would have to consider the situation at the time of the death.

Finally, under this category, a so-called common law spouse does not have the right to claim. A co-habitee could possibly make a claim under paragraph (e).

Paragraph (b) gives a former spouse the right to apply. However it was pointed out in *Re Fullard* [1981] 2 All ER 796 that applicants under this category would be rare since the issue of provision should have been considered on the divorce. It is particularly important to address the question on the divorce in view of the change made by s. 18A, Wills Act 1837, which revokes gifts to a spouse in the will in the event of a divorce. However, although rare, applications are not ruled out and one situation is where, e.g., a wife has failed to pursue her full rights for maintenance on the divorce, as in *Re W* (1975) where the wife was, to quote the court, 'of a gentle and compliant disposition'.

Paragraph (c) — any child of the deceased includes illegitimate children and a child *en ventre sa mère* (or wherever the child takes its holidays!), but not a step-child. Unlike the inheritance (Family Provision) Act 1938, there are no age or other restrictions, so one could have an application by an adult, able-bodied child. For example, in *Re Christie* (1979) Ch 168 an adult son successfully obtained an order which, in effect, recouped a devise for him where his mother had failed to change her will after selling the property, which was the subject matter of the original gift, to him (thereby adeeming the devise). Provision for the adult child can be a recurring theme in questions and the decision in *Re Christie* was criticised by the Court of Appeal in *Re Coventry* [1980] Ch 461 where unsympathetic comments were made about adult, able-bodied children entertaining applications. In addition the Court of Appeal in *Re Coventry* pointed out that the object of the Inheritance (Provision for Family and Dependants) Act 1975 in the categories excluding the spouse was to consider reasonable provision, meaning maintenance, and not to correct legacies.

The step child is included in paragraph (d) — child of the family. This paragraph would also include a child of the deceased's family such as an orphaned nephew. You will appreciate that one must look for evidence of more than mere affection. How does one assess whether a person is a 'child of the family'? Section 3(3) refers to 'assumption of responsibility for the maintenance of the applicant'; whether, in assuming responsibility, the deceased did so knowing the applicant was not his own child. Also one should consider whether anyone else should bear the responsibility of maintaining the applicant.

A leading case which requires careful study is the judgment of the Court of Appeal in *Re Leach* [1985] 2 All ER 754. Although each case turns on its own facts, this case is unusual in involving an application by a 55 year-old step-daughter. The application was successful. The main judgment was given by Slade LJ who said, at page 760:

> the legislature cannot have contemplated that the mere display of affection, kindness of hospitality by a step-parent towards a step-child will by itself involve the treatment of the step-parent of the step-child as a child of the family in relation to the marriage . . . Something more is needed: reasonable step-parents can usually be expected to behave in a civilised and friendly manner towards their step-children, if only for the sake of the spouse . . . What more then is needed? Counsel for the defendant submitted treatment by one person or another as a child of the family must necessarily involve the treatment of that other person as 'an unfledged person'.

Slade LJ said this had superficial attractions particularly in relation to a young child. He then went on to quote from the judgment of Booth J in *Re Callaghan* [1984] 3 All ER 790 at 793 where references were made as to confidences of property and financial affairs between the parties. *Re Callaghan* is another leading case which should be carefully studied. Again this involved a successful application by an adult step-child where there was a close relation of care between step-child and deceased. Both judgments should be read carefully for, given statistics on re-marriage, the numbers of stepchildren are increasing.

Paragraph (e) — any person, not within the other categories, who, immediately before the death of the deceased, was being maintained wholly or partly by the deceased. This category represents the biggest departure from the restrictive categories under the 1938 legislation. Labelled 'the mistresses' charter' it gave recognition for the first time to a possible application by a co-habitee.

Consider carefully what the applicant needs to establish in order to prove *locus standi*. The applicant must not come within any other category; the deceased must have been maintaining the applicant or making a substantial contribution towards the applicant's needs immediately before the death; the deceased must not have been receiving full and valuable consideration for the maintenance and there must be some assumption of responsibility towards the applicant.

Careful study of the cases shows that the parties need not be related nor live under the same roof. Maintenance, though expressed in monetary terms could be, for example, the provision of accommodation, as in *Re Wilkinson* (1978) Fam 22. If the parties have reached an understanding, a form of bargain where each agrees to bear responsibilities, then this would appear to negate the right to apply under paragraph (e). The parties may be both working individuals who decide to co-habit and share equally the costs of accommodation, food and creature comforts. They may be an older couple, perhaps both widowed, who do not want to re-marry but know that two together can live more cheaply than two apart and know they would be happy to share a common roof for companionship. The leading decisions on this preliminary question of *locus standi* under (e) are both by the Court of Appeal; *Jelley* v *Iliffe* [1981] Fam 128 and *Bishop* v *Plumley* [1991] 1 All ER 236.

The meaning of 'was being maintained' in s. 1(1)(e) is explained in s. 1(3):

> . . . if the deceased, otherwise than for full valuable consideration, was making a substantial contribution in money or money's worth towards the reasonable needs of that person.

In *Re Beaumont* [1980] 1 All ER 266 and in *Jelley* v *Iliffe*, the courts have interpreted s. 1(3) as an exclusive definition of paragraph (e), that is, reading '(only) if the deceased, otherwise than for full valuable consideration . . .'. See the dictum of Stephenson LJ in *Jelley* v *Iliffe*. Stephenson LJ directed the court to look at the settled basis or arrangement between the parties in the period before the death and not to the actual, perhaps fluctuating, variation which could exist immediately before the death. The words 'full valuable consideration' in s. 1(3) are not confined to valuable consideration under a contract but apply whenever full valuable consideration is given.

Section 3(4) requires the court to consider the extent and the basis upon which the deceased assumed responsibility for the maintenance of the applicant, and the length of time for which the deceased discharged that responsibility. Megarry VC in *Re Beaumont* said there must be evidence of proof of assumption of responsibility. Stephenson LJ and Goff LJ in *Jelley* v *Iliffe* refused to follow this line of interpretation and concluded that the bare fact of maintenance raises a presumption of assumption of responsibility. Stephenson LJ in *Jelley* v *Iliffe* went on to say:

> To discover whether the deceased was making (a substantial) contribution the court has to balance what she was contributing against what he was contributing, and, if there is any doubt about the balance tipping in favour of hers (the deceased) being the greater contribution, the matter must in my opinion, go to trial. If however, the balance is bound to come down in favour of his being the greater contribution, or if the contributions are clearly equal, there is no dependency of him on her, either because she depended upon him or there was mutual dependency between them. Then the application should be struck out as bound to fail.

The courts recognise that circumstances can change. What set out to be equal contributions in a relationship can turn into dependence. Maintenance is not a matter for mathematical calculations. In *Bishop* v *Plumley* (1991) Butler-Sloss LJ said that one should look at the situation in the round and adopt a common-sense approach. It is difficult to see any error in the law which gave rise to the appeal in *Bishop* v *Plumley*; however the decision does appear to reflect a more favourable, flexible approach by the courts to claims by co-habitees. Also bear in mind the Law Commission's recommendation in its report on intestate reform, No. 187, that co-habitees should not have to be called upon to prove prior dependence in making a claim for reasonable provision.

The Law Commission in its recommendations rejected the idea of a statutory minimum period of co-habitation. However, the length of time the relationship has subsisted is clearly an important factor in considering an award. As Arnond J pointed out in *Re Wilkinson* [1978] 1 All ER 221 the onus of bringing the applicant within paragraph (e) rests squarely with the applicant. The applicant must demonstrate that he or she was being maintained by the deceased. Section 1(3) makes it clear maintenance and full valuable consideration are not simply, or even primarily, matters of the payment of money. Nor do the provisions merely require the court to consider, as well as money, those goods and services which can be easily given a monetary value. The value of such things as companionship, rent-free accommodation with the deceased and help about the house have to be taken into account. Stephenson LJ in *Jelley* v *Iliffe* said: 'I have no doubt that the provision of free accommodation in these times is a substantial contribution to the needs of the accommodated'. In *Bishop* v *Plumley* the deceased was taken to have made a substantial contribution to the maintenance of the applicant by providing a secure home for the applicant.

A final note of caution before we leave the preliminary question of *locus standi*. Paragraph (e) refers to maintenance 'immediately before the death of the deceased'. Clearly one does not simply look at the situation at the death but would consider the normal, habitual state. Megarry VC in *Re Beaumont* (1980) gives an example where the parties have lived together through a settled relationship but before the death they are separated because, in the final period, the deceased is hospitalised. This would not preclude a claim. However, where the deceased has made a conscious decision to break the relationship before the death, then the applicant will not be able to sustain a claim. See, for example, the judgment of Wood J in *Kourky* v *Lusher, The Times*, 9 December 1981.

In questions on these preliminary issues look for points concerning the more difficult areas of *locus standi*, in particular, the dependant within (e) and the child of the family concept within (d). Once *locus standi* is established the next major hurdle is to establish whether reasonable provision has been made for the applicant. Remember that these provisions do not simply apply where the deceased has left a will, for application can be made on intestacy or partial intestacy.

A major change made by the 1975 Act was to create two standards: (i) reasonable provision for the spouse — broadly, what would the spouse receive if the parties were divorcing at the time of the death? and (ii) reasonable provision in all other cases, meaning maintenance.

The spouse

Section 1(2)(a) says 'provision as would be reasonable in all the circumstances'. This must be read in conjunction with s. 3(2) that the starting point is the amount which the applicant could be expected to have received on a divorce. However, simply proving one is the lawful spouse does not necessarily mean that a substantial award would be made. The parties may have lived apart for a considerable period of time. The deceased may have had a long standing, settled relationship, with someone else. Where the spouses are judicially separated, the criterion for an application is one of maintenance and not the spouse standard. However, the court does have a discretion under s. 14 to apply the spouse standard to judicially separated spouses or to former spouses who have not re-married. In practice it is likely that the issue of provision would have been considered in the earlier deliberations following the separation. The Court of Appeal in *Re Fullard* [1981] 2 All ER 796 said that such applications would be rare. One should look for a substantial change in circumstances which could trigger an application to the court to exercise its discretion.

The leading cases on the interpretation of the spouse standard are *Re Besterman* [1984] 2 All ER 656 and *Re Bunning* [1984] 3 All ER 1. *Re Besterman* is a good example of a claim where the deceased was not deliberately ignoring a dependant, in this case his spouse, but miscalculating the cost of the lifestyle to which they had become accustomed where the deceased husband was a millionaire. Oliver LJ said that the starting point was the likely provision on divorce:

The figure resulting from a s. 25, Matrimonial Causes Act 1973 application is merely one of the factors to which the court is to have regard and the overriding consideration is what is 'reasonable in the circumstances', it is however a very important consideration and one which the statute goes out of the way to bring to the court's attention. If therefore the provision which the court finds to be reasonable under the 1975 Act turns out to be very widely at variance with the figure which might be expected to be achieved on a divorce, one is immediately driven to ask what regard their trial judge did in fact pay to it . . .

The court, in considering the spouse standard, should look at the length of the marriage and the relationship between them. The court will ask what contribution the applicant has made to the welfare of the family, and consider the age of the surviving spouse. Although the court in *Re Besterman* stressed that each case depends upon its own facts, the guidelines referred to were followed in *Re Bunning*. In *Moody* v *Stevenson, The Independent*, 17 September 1991, the Court of Appeal said that the test as to reasonable provision for the surviving spouse was objective, that is, to be decided by the court, and was not whether the testator acted reasonably in making the dispositions. The objective in the case of an application by a widow (or, as in *Moody*, a widower) was that the acceptable minimum posthumous provision for a surviving spouse should correspond as closely as possible to the inchoate rights enjoyed by the spouse in the deceased's lifetime by virtue of his or her entitlement under the matrimonial law. There would, however, be occasions when the objective was unattainable. Here, the Court of Appeal allowed an appeal by a widower, the second husband, who was claiming entitlement to continue to live in the house owned by the testatrix deceased, where the testatrix had willed the property to her step-daughter from her first marriage. The court accepted that a family judge would probably direct a settlement of the property on terms which would give the applicant a right of occupancy. However brief a marriage may be the court will recognise, in considering an award, the fact that the parties entered into the marriage contract rather than co-habited.

Under s. 3(5) the court is to take account of the facts at the date of the hearing. In *Rajabally* v *Rajabally* [1987] 17 Fam Law 314 the court ruled that it was not entitled to take account of legally unenforceable assurances given by other beneficiaries under the will.

The maintenance standard — s. 1(2)(b)

'. . . the introduction of an expanded class of potential applicants does not of itself point to the adoption of any different approach to the exercise of the discretion, which remains restricted, to "reasonable provision for maintenance" . . .' per Oliver LJ in *Re Coventry* [1979] 3 All ER 815.

There is no statutory definition of maintenance. One needs to consider the case law to elicit principles. Maintenance does not mean subsistence (*Re Christie* [1979] 1 All ER 546). The concept denotes payments which directly or indirectly enable the applicant to discharge the recurrent costs of daily living. This would generally exclude substantial capital benefit. See, for example, dicta in *Re Dennis* [1981] 2 All ER 140 which concerned an application by a profligate son who was caught on the hook of estate duty liability arising from substantial gifts *inter vivos*.

The level of maintenance is not to be determined solely in relation to the applicant's financial position but regard must be had to the person's social position and station in life; see *Re Inns* [1947] 2 All ER 308. One factor is the level of support and encouragement given by the deceased to the applicant to adopt a particular lifestyle; see *Malone* v *Harrison* [1979] 1 WLR 1353. In *Re Christie* the court said that maintenance may denote the well being, health and financial security of the applicant and his immediate family even if the only way this can be ensured is by the provision of capital. This decision was criticised by the Court of Appeal in *Re Coventry* where it was emphasised that the purpose is to provide maintenance and not to correct a will by providing legacies.

The test as to reasonable provision is an objective one (s. 3(5)) to be determined at the date of the application. Clearly one has to consider the question, 'has reasonable provision been made at the date of death in order to consider making an application in the first place?'. However, once an application to the court has been made, the timing of the objective test means that the court will be able to take account of supervening events. Suppose, for example, a father leaves his daughter a block of shares believing their market value and yield would adequately provide for the daughter after his death. If the shares do not prove to be as valuable following the death (they could be shares in a family company where the death has an adverse effect on the value), then the fall in value and prospects for the fund could be considered fully at the date of the application.

The approach — a case study

Let us pause and consider the following case study. Four years ago John left his wife, Kate, after twelve years of marriage and went to live with Susan in the apartment he provided for her which is in his name. He has paid maintenance, by an informal agreement, to Kate, their son Alec and a contribution towards the school fees for Beth, Kate's daughter from her previous marriage to Lionel deceased. John has now died and his will, after leaving legacies of £10,000 each to Kate and Susan and £5,000 to Alec, leaves the remainder of the estate, value in excess of £300,000, to a named charity.

You are asked to consider the claims, if any, which could be made by all those named, all of whom survive John.

Your preliminary steps would be to advise the survivors whether they had *locus standi*. Clearly Kate, as surviving spouse, has a claim. The maintenance payments are not secured by court order, therefore, without judicial separation, the merits of Kate's claim will be judged according to the spouse standard. Alec, as John's child, has *locus standi*. Beth would have to establish that she is a 'child of the family' and Susan would need to show dependency within paragraph (e). On would then consider the guidelines on factors to consider for the spouse standard, citing *Re Besterman* (1984) and the related authorities. In the case of all the other potential claimants the criterion is one of maintenance.

The court is not obliged to make an order but will have regard to certain factors in accordance with s. 3 in deciding whether to make an award to a particular applicant. Consider the factors carefully and do not present these simply as a list but demonstrate, through your knowledge of the cases, how relevant the factors are to the particular applicant.

The factors

The court will have regard to the following:

(1) **The moral obligation owed by the deceased**. Moral obligation is not a pre-requisite, merely a factor. The Court of Appeal in *Re Coventry* said that the mere fact that a claimant finds himself in necessitous circumstances is not sufficient to establish a moral claim. Moral obligation was an overriding factor in both *Re Callaghan* (1984) and *Re Leach* (1985). Note the judgment in *Re Ducksbury* [1966] 1 WLR 1226 which shows that moral obligation can switch from one party to another.

(2) **The financial position of the applicant** is clearly an important factor. The court will consider whether the applicant is young enough and able to resume employment. The approach is not dissimilar to industrial injury cases, see, for example, the calculations made by the court in *Malone* v *Harrison* [1979] 1 WLR 1353.

(3) **The financial position of other applicants and the beneficiaries under the will** or intestacy. The courts have taken a different attitude where estate assets have been left to charity rather than e.g., an individual who may have a greater moral claim to the testator's bounty; see, for example, *Re Parkinson (dec'd)* (1975) LS Gaz 29 October.

(4) **The size of the net estate.** Assets may not be in a realisable form. Also, the courts have shown a reluctance to make orders in small estates, criticising applications in view of the risks of costs absorbing assets. *Re Parkinson* is an example in point where on the appeal the costs had risen so the main asset, the house, had to be sold to meet the costs.

(5) **Any physical or mental disability of an applicant or a beneficiary.** The courts will disregard the effect which a likely award would have upon the receipt of State benefits such as income support, see dicta in *Re Collins* [1990] 2 All ER 47.

(6) **Section 3(1)(g) gives the court the power to consider any other relevant matter.** This has included, for example, the source of the deceased's funds. In *Re Sivyer* [1967] 3 All ER 429 the fact that a large proportion of the

estate came from the value of the house purchased with the assistance of the savings of the applicant's mother, the deceased's second wife, was taken into account. In *Re W* (1975) 119 Sol Jo owing to the wife's compliant nature, she had not pursued a legitimate claim for maintenance on the separation, thereby enabling the husband to accumulate a greater amount of capital; this, too, was a factor to be considered by the court.

It is under this head that the court will consider any reasons given by the deceased as to why provision has not been made. Section 21 allows the admission of written or oral statements in accordance with s. 2, Civil Evidence Act 1968. However, the court will not accept these statements at face value but will enquire as to the substance, see dicta in *Re Clarke* [1968] 1 WLR 415.

Questions will generally concentrate upon the issue of *locus standi* and the merits of the respective parties. However, one must have regard to the time limit under s. 4. The rule is substantive and must be engraved on the heart of every budding property practitioner, or else it is a case of dusting down the insurance policy and re-reading *Ross* v *Caunters* (1980). Application to the court must be made within six months of the issue of the first grant to the estate. The rule is substantive and not merely procedural; the courts are very reluctant to extend the time limit. *Re Salmon* [1980] 3 All ER 532 should be studied for the dangers of lack of communication and delay, and the clear exposition of guidelines concerning applications out of time given by Megarry VC and considered with approval in *Re Dennis* (1981), the saga of the profligate son.

In *Whyte* v *Ticehurst* [1986] 2 All ER 158 the court ruled that an application under the 1975 Act is a personal action, therefore the right to apply dies with the applicant and the right to pursue the claim does not pass to the applicant's personal representatives. Also consider the decision of the court in *Re Basham (dec'd)* [1987] 1 All ER 405 which illustrates a novel alternative approach. In this case the applicant successfully established a claim to a cottage based upon proprietary estoppel. Note, however, dicta in *Layton* v *Martin* [1986] 2 FLR 277 which suggest that such a claim is confined to specific property.

The property available for an award

Section 25(1) should be studied carefully; in particular, note the extensions to the meaning of 'net estate' to include, for example, *donatio mortis causa* and property held on a joint tenancy. Section 9(1) enables the court to override the right of survivorship to the joint tenant in making an award. Also consider the wide powers given to the court to make a variety of orders under s. 2 including, for example, the power to order acquisition and transfer of property and the variation of a marriage settlement.

Anti-avoidance

In studying the 1975 Act three major changes stand out in comparison with the 1938 legislation: (1) the extension in the categories of claimant, in particular paragraph (e); (2) the difference in the basis of the award for the surviving spouse; and (3) the introduction of anti-avoidance provisions. In some estates application will be considered where the testator has miscalculated the cost of maintaining a standard of living to which the party has become accustomed, as in *Re Besterman*; or, there has been a supervening event which has altered the calculation of assets in the estate, such as the failure of the loan re-payment in *Re Goodwin* [1968] 3 All ER 12. However, there remains the possibility that some testators will take deliberate steps to reduce the possibility of a successful application for provision.

Order for provision are out of the net estate of the deceased. Broadly, two methods could be adopted to reduce the chances of a successful claim. One method would be to give away property prior to death. This has the effect of reducing the net estate and can have tax attractions. Alternatively the deceased could seek to impose liabilities on the estate which would have to be dealt with before the net estate could be calculated.

Section 10 is aimed at countering the person who gives away property prior to death, by enabling the claiming back of dispositions made within six years of the death. In order to make a successful re-claim, the applicant must show that the dispositions were not made for full, valuable consideration and that they had been made with a view to avoiding a claim under the Act. The court will be ready to infer an intention to defeat the Act. Proof is on the balance of probabilities and the intention to defeat does not have to be the sole reason for making the disposition. The court will inquire as to the intention behind the disposition. In *Re Bunning* an attempt was made to claw back a gift to charity made within six years of the death, but this was rejected when evidence showed that both parties had acceded to the gift. The court can make an order under s. 10 against the donee to provide a specified sum of money or other property as part of an order to provide reasonable provision. In *Re Dawkins* (1986) 2 FLR 360 the deceased died insolvent, having sold his house worth £27,000 to his daughter from a previous marriage, for £100 some fifteen months before his death. The intention was to defeat a claim under the Act. The court ordered the recipient daughter to provide £10,000 by way of lump sum provision for the applicant, who was the deceased's second wife. An order can be made against the donee even if the donee has disposed of the property, although the value is then taken as at the date of disposal rather than the date of death.

Enjoyment of the property after the disposition will not necessarily mean that the property can be made the subject of a s. 10 order. For example, if

Arthur gives Betty his house, but Arthur continues to live in the house and more than six years elapse from the date of the deed of gift, the property cannot be clawed back. Compare the situation where Arthur takes a life interest in a settlement which he creates more than six years before his death, but where he retains a power of appointment over the property. The property will form part of his net estate at death.

Section 11 deals with the alternative method of increasing liabilities by deliberately creating a claim upon the estate. Note here, as regards contracts, that there is no six year cut off. The law recognises that one can contract to leave property by will (*Synge* v *Synge* [1894] QB 466, *Hammersley* v *De Biel* (1845) 12 Cl & Fin 45). Suppose the testator enters into such a contract but does not execute the will, thereby rendering the contract actionable. The person seeking to enforce the contract claims as a creditor therefore the claim must be settled before the net estate can be determined. Study the facts in *Schaefer* v *Schuhmann* [1972] 1 All ER 621 where the housekeeper established a claim to the house based upon part performance. If the case was heard under the 1975 Act, the applicant daughter would have to establish that the devise of the house by the codicil and the establishment of the contract was intended to avoid a claim under the Act.

Section 11 applies to contracts to pass property on death. A contract to transfer property during life, for example an *inter vivos* covenant to pay a sum of money, is outside the Act. However, the word of Lord Cross in *Schaefer* v *Schuhmann* should be heeded:

> . . . whether contracts made by a testator not with a view to excluding the jurisdiction of the court under this Act but in the normal course of arranging his affairs in his lifetime should be liable to be wholly or partially set aside by the court . . . is a question of social policy on which different people may reasonably take different views.

The court will have regard to the circumstances surrounding the disposition or contract, the relationship of the donor to the donee and the respective financial circumstances of the parties and the applicants in the estate.

Problem

Consider the following problem concerning possible claims under the 1975 Act, and the suggested framework answer.

William died two months ago appointing you executor and leaving his estate to two named charities. William is survived by his wife, Kate, whom he married 20 years ago (they separated four years ago); their sons, James and Peter; Lizzie, Kate's illegitimate daughter out of a brief affair with a sailor and Tara, William's mistress. Tara lives at 'Greygables', the riverside property William purchased for Tara three years ago.

William had paid for Lizzie's education at boarding school and regularly gave her presents. William had always said that Jill, James's wife (a particular favourite of William) would have his London flat. Peter is presently boarding at Winchester and William has been paying the fees. Tara worked freelance as an advertising accounts manager but stopped work at William's request when she went to live at 'Greygables'.

Kate has owned a successful interior design business for the past eight years, obtaining most of her clients through the building conversions carried out by the firm belonging to William. After the death of William the design contracts cease. You have received a letter from a friend of Kate's, requesting an 'ex gratia payment' for Kate out of the estate.

The estate is valued at £320,000 at death.

Consider the possible claims which could be made under the Inheritance (Provision for Family and Dependants) Act 1975 and the response you would make to the letter of request.

The Inheritance (Provision for Family and Dependants) Act 1975 established new categories of persons who could possibly claim against the estate of the deceased where it is considered that the deceased has failed to make reasonable provision for persons by his will, intestacy or a combination of both.

In order to establish a claim under the 1975 Act an applicant must show that the deceased has died domiciled in England and Wales; the applicant has the *locus standi* to apply and the deceased has failed to make reasonable provision for the applicant.

Assuming William meets the domiciliary requirement, who could apply in his estate, given that he has left all his property to charity? Kate, as his surviving spouse — s. 1(1)(a); James and Peter as children of the deceased — s. 1(1)(c); Lizzie, if she could establish she is a 'child of the family' within sub-paragraph (d) and Tara, if she can prove she was dependent upon William immediately before his death — s. 1(1)(e).

In the case of Lizzie she would have to prove more than merely friendly relations and the giving of presents. She would have to establish a recognition or assumption of filial responsibilities by William towards Lizzie in order for her to establish that she is a 'child of the family'; see the dictum of Slade LJ in *Re Leach* (1988).

Tara would have to establish dependence upon William immediately before his death (*Kourkey* v *Lusher*). The concept of dependence can include the provision of a roof over one's head rather than simply monetary payments; *Re Wilkinson* (1978). The courts will look for evidence of a bargain between the parties based upon consideration which would deny the existence of dependence. Where there is no evidence of an agreement on dependence. One looks for mutual or individual dependence. One looks at the situation in the round to assess the contribution of either party; *Bishop* v *Plumley* (1990) and *Jelley* v *Iliffe* (1981). Given that William purchased the house for Tara and Tara gave up a source of income at William's request, it is likely that Tara could establish *locus standi*.

Reasonable provision is divided into two categories: (1) provision for the surviving spouse, the divorce standard; s. 1(2)(a), s. 3(2); and (2) the maintenance standard; s. 1(2)(b). Does the surviving spouse standard apply to Kate? One would have to enquire, given that they are separated, whether there is a decree of judicial separation which was in force at the date of the death. Despite the decree, spouses remain *prima facie* entitled to apply. However, they may agree at the time of the decree that neither spouse will make an application. This will not prevent an order being made, unless the decree is still in force at the date of death and the separation has continued until the death. Where the separation has continued to the death, but application is made by Kate, the standard is the maintenance standard. However, the court has a discretion to apply the divorce standard; s. 14.

Kate will be in a stronger position if she can establish a claim based upon the divorce standard. The Court of Appeal in *Re Besterman* (1984) indicated guidelines (though stressed that each case depends on the particular facts) in calculating an award. These include the length of the marriage; the nature of the relationship, whether it was a happy one; the circumstances of a separation; the standard of life the couple had attained; the age of the surviving spouse and the likelihood of her gaining employment. These points were adopted by the court in *Re Bunning* (1984).

In the case of other potential applicants, and possibly Kate, depending upon the separation, the basis of provision is one of maintenance; s. 1(2)(b). 'Maintenance' is not defined in the Act but the concept denotes payments which directly or indirectly enable the applicant to discharge the recurrent costs of daily living; *Re Dennis* (1981). What standard of life had the applicant come to expect (*Re Inns* (1947)) or been encouraged to adopt (*Malone* v *Harrison* (1979))? Maintenance may denote the well being, health and financial security of the applicant (*Re Christie* (1979)).

The test as to reasonable provision is objective, to be applied at the date of the hearing; s. 3(5). Clearly consideration as to the merits of the claim has to be made at the time of the death, for the applicant must make application to the court within six months from the issue of the original grant to the estate; s. 4; see also *Re Salmon* (1981). However, in looking at the situation at the date of the hearing, the court can take into account supervening events such as the ending of Kate's design contracts; see *Re Goodwin* (1968). The response to the request for an ex gratia payment would be for Kate to make a formal application to the court for reasonable provision; see *Re Salmon*. To make such a payment without fully considering the merits and possible claims of other applicants, could render the personal representatives personally liable to the beneficiaries.

In considering whether to make an award, the court has regard to a number of factors which influence whether an award would be made and the extent of the award; s. 3. These factors include a moral obligation owed by the deceased to the applicant; the financial circumstances of the applicant; the size of the net estate and the merits of other applicants, as well as consideration of the beneficiaries under the will. The courts have indicated more sympathy for individuals applying where the beneficiary is a charity, rather than another individual; see dicta in *Millward* v *Shenton* [1972] 2 All ER 1025.

James is married to Jill. There are no details as to his circumstances. There is no age limit to an application by a child (*Re Christie*) although merits will vary where the child is already established in life; *Re Coventry* (1979). Peter, on the other hand, is still at school thereby strengthening a claim for maintenance provision to meet recurring costs and expenses (see dicta in *Re Dennis*). Jill would not appear to have *locus standi* under the Act. However, it would depend upon the representations regarding the London flat as to whether she could establish a claim based upon proprietary estoppel, as in *Re Basham* (1987).

The court has wide powers in the types of order which can be made out of the net estate (s. 25(1)) to the successful applicant. Under s. 2 the court can make orders for periodic payments, lump sums and order the transfer, acquisition or settlement of property.

Question

Reasonable provision in cases other than the surviving spouse standard refers to the 'maintenance standard'. How has 'maintenance' been interpreted by the courts?

Comment

In considering the question has the testator made reasonable financial provision the legislation sets out a two-stage process. One asks, has the will or intestacy of the deceased or a combination or both failed to make reasonable financial provision for the applicant. If the answer is yes, then the court considers what would amount to reasonable provision for the applicant. There are two standards of provision, the surviving spouse standard (s. 1(2)(a) of the Inheritance (Provision for Family and Dependants) Act 1975) and the maintenance standard.

Section 1(2)(b) of the 1975 Act defines the maintenance standard as 'such financial provision as it would be reasonable in all the circumstances of the case for the applicant to receive for his maintenance'. The word 'maintenance' is not defined in the Act. One therefore has to turn to the decisions of the courts to obtain guidance as to the meaning of the word. Maintenance does not mean merely providing the applicant with the bare necessities of life, so as to keep the applicant at subsistence level. See, for example, dicta in *Re Coventry* [1980] Ch 461. In *Re E* [1966] 1 WLR 709 the court said the purpose of the 1938 Act (where the maintenance standard was the only measure) was not to require the deceased to keep applicants 'above the breadline'. Browne-Wilkinson J in *Re Dennis* [1981] 2 All ER 140 said maintenance connotes provision which, directly or indirectly, enables the applicant to 'discharge the cost of his daily living at whatever standard of living is appropriate to him'. Here, an application by a dissolute son in the estate of his father failed where the application was prompted by a demand for a substantial death duty liability arising from a gift *inter vivos*. The out of time application was rejected on the basis that maintenance does not generally include the provision of a substantial capital benefit. The court did recognise however that the payment of debts to enable an applicant to carry on a profit making profession or business may be for maintenance. The level of support is not to be determined simply by reference to the applicant's financial position but regard must also be paid to his social position and station, see the judgment in *Re Inns* [1947] 2 All ER 308. The level of support can also be determined by the standard of life the deceased encouraged the applicant to adopt, as in *Malone v Harrison* [1979] 1 WLR 1353. Here, the applicant was the mistress of the deceased and had been given over a period of years two apartments, jewellery and money.

In *Re Christie* [1979] 1 All ER 546 the deputy judge said that maintenance may denote the well-being, health and financial security of the applicant and his immediate family, even if the only way this can be done is by the provision of capital. Here, an adult son successfully applied for a property transfer to apparently correct the omission by the deceased, his mother, in failing to alter her will after selling the house she had devised to him and moving to a smaller property. The judgment was criticised by the Court of Appeal in *Re Coventry* where Goff LJ expressed concern at the very broad interpretation of maintenance, in equating the term simply with 'well being' or 'benefit'. He said the purpose of the 1975 Act was not to correct legacies.

The term 'maintenance' connotes an income provision, to enable the applicant to continue, within reason, an acquired lifestyle. Although the court has wide power to order, for example, lump sum payments and the making of property transfer orders in ordering reasonable provision be made from the estate, the criterion upon which the order is made is one of income provision.

EIGHT

LEGACIES

Introduction

Henry, by his will, leaves 'my gold watch to my brother, Oliver; 5,000 shares in Rockon Limited to my sister, Paula; £1,000 out of my account at Barclays plc to my nephew, Michael and the remainder of my estate to my wife, Linda'.

These provisions read clearly enough. However, what claim, if any, does Oliver have if the gold watch no longer forms part of the assets at the death of Henry? Perhaps Henry has sold the watch, or it has been stolen. Suppose before the death of Henry the shares in Rockon Limited are sold and the balance in the account at Barclays at the death is £500. What claims, if any, can Paula and Michael make against the estate?

To answer these popular examination questions and important practical issues, the different types of legacy must be distinguished, their respective characteristics and effects understood. So often students in tackling gift questions fail to build up the answer by explaining the significance of the different categories. Why is it important to distinguish between the specific and the general legacy, to identify the demonstrative legacy or residuary gift? The reason is consideration of the effects of ademption and abatement.

The specific legacy

A reference in a will to some part of the assets of the testator, made in such a way as to distinguish the asset from the remaining assets in the estate, would make the gift specific. So in the gift Henry makes to Oliver, the gift of the watch is a specific legacy. Henry refers to 'my gold watch' saying, in effect, 'you know the gold watch I own, I want you (Oliver) to have it after my death'. A specific legacy is often identified by the prefix 'my' but this is not conclusive. The categorisation may appear to be straightforward in the case of an identifiable personal item such as a watch, however, the situation is not clear when, for example, shares, are the subject matter of the gift.

You see officer, my theory is that this is the remains of A. Batement and A.
Demption was driving the train

The characteristics of the specific legacy were considered by Jessel MR in *Bothamley* v *Sherson* (1875) LR 20 Eq 304, when the court held that a bequest of '. . . all my shares or stock in the Midland Railway Company' was specific. Jessel MR said that the asset must be distinguished from the whole in such a way as to make the asset or assets stand apart from the remainder of the property in the estate. This could be achieved by saying 'the black horses I now have'.

The danger in deciding that a gift is specific is the application of the doctrine of ademption. If the asset no longer forms part of the assets of the deceased at death, the gift has been adeemed and the beneficiary cannot take the property. So, in the case of Oliver, he would not be entitled to the gold watch, for it no longer forms part of the estate. This applies irrespective of the reason why Henry no longer has the watch. Henry could have given it away, or it may have been stolen, but whatever the reason, the asset is no longer there. However, the application of ademption is not a pre-condition of deciding that a gift is specific. Jessel MR in *Bothamley* v *Sherson* gave the example '. . . the black horses of which I shall be possessed at death'. The gift example is no less specific and ademption will not apply, for the point in time to ascertain the gift is immediately before the death of the testator. The courts have shown a reluctance to hold gifts to be specific in view of the effect of ademption, for example, where the change in the nature of a shareholding is considered to be one of form and not substance as in *Re Willcocks* [1921] 2 Ch 327. The problems in gifts of shares are considered later in this chapter.

The decision as to whether or not the gift is specific turns upon the intention of the testator. *Re Eve* [1956] 3 All ER 321 is an interesting example where there was a gift of an option to buy shares in a particular company at their par value. Roxburgh J held that the gift was not specific for the gift merely gave the beneficiary a right to buy shares. Was the specific gift the difference in the value of the shares from par value to market value? 'No', said Roxburgh J, for this aspect had not been distinguished by the testator.

General legacies

A general legacy does not specifically identify the particular item of property bequeathed. 'A gold watch to Ringo', '£1,000 to Sheila' are general gifts. The testator has not pointed to a particular gold watch. The assets do not therefore have to form part of the estate assets at death. The gift acts as a direction to the personal representatives to acquire a gold watch for Ringo and to give £1,000 to Sheila. In *Re Connor* [1948] 1 Ch 628 the testator gave his son 'ten thousand preference shares . . . in J & K O'Connor Ltd.'. At death there were 9,000 preference shares in the estate. Roxburgh J held that the gift was general. He pointed out that the possessive noun 'my' was not used and, a significant point in Roxburgh J's view, the testator had never owned 10,000 preference shares in the company. The line is a fine one for Roxburgh J pointed out that if the testator had left 9,000 preference shares, he would have held the gift to be specific.

The advantage of the general legacy is that it does not fall victim to ademption, the danger is abatement. If there are insufficient funds to meet general legacies, they will abate ratably according to value. So, for example, if Henry left two general pecuniary gifts of £2,000 and £1,000 but there was only £1,000 left after the settlement of all liabilities, then the beneficiaries would share the £1,000 in the ratio 2:1.

If the property does not form part of the assets at death, the gift serves as a direction to the personal representatives to acquire the property for the beneficiary. In the case of the gift to Henry's sister, Paula, it is debatable whether the gift is specific (see *Barthomley* v *Sherson*) or general (see *Re O'Connor*). If it is general, the personal representatives will have to acquire sufficient shares to bring the gift up to 5,000, or offer Paula the monetary equivalent. This pre-supposes that the shares are obtainable. If the company has failed, then neither the shares nor their monetary equivalent can be obtained and the gift could not take effect; see *Re Gray* (1887) 36 Ch D 205.

The demonstrative legacy

The demonstrative legacy is often described as a 'hybrid' in that there are two 'bites'. 'It is in the nature of a general legacy but there is a particular fund pointed out to satisfy it', said Lord Thurlow in *Ashburner* v *Macguire* (1786) 2 Bro CC 108. In the case of the gift to Michael, if there is only £500 in the account with Barclays, then Michael will be entitled to the account and claim along with the other general legatees for the balance in order to afford to buy Arnold, the parrot. (Not the parrot again — yes! One might say that Arnold is more fun than distinguishing legacies!)

Pecuniary legacies

As the name suggests, these are gifts of money. They are usually general, e.g., '£200 to Chris'; they can be demonstrative, as in the gift to Michael, they may even be specific; e.g., 'the £700 Sam owes to me I leave to Tessa'.

Residuary gifts

A residuary gift is one which gives the beneficiary all that remains of the estate after the funeral, testamentary, administration expenses, debts, other liabilities and gifts under the will have been met. Note that there is a different meaning to the word 'residue' when we consider the administration of the solvent estate in chapter 10. Also, where a residuary gift fails, for example, if Linda pre-deceases Henry with the result that the gift to her lapses, in the absence of a gift over, there would be a partial intestacy. The example which opened this chapter clearly referred to 'residue'. Watch in questions of this type where, e.g., Henry's will had read '. . . and the remainder of my effects' or, '. . . all my moneys' . . . to Linda. What Henry means is a matter of construction for the court, considered in chapter 9.

Ademption

The question as to whether there has been ademption is difficult to answer in relation to property which is capable of reduction and addition in the period from the date of the will until the date on which the will becomes effective, the date of death. This is particularly the case in relation to gifts of shares.

The distinction between specific and general in relation to legacies is not an easy one to draw. In the litigation the subject matter of the gift has either been reduced, or has gone from the estate entirely; therefore, if the gift is specific there is ademption either wholly or in part. There are a number of cases which illustrate the difficulties.

The courts will try to uphold a gift wherever possible. A good example in the construction of gifts is *Re Gage* [1934] Ch 536; note how the court used the presence of the word 'and' to separate a gift of government stock from a prior specific gift, thereby enabling the court to conclude that the gift of the stock was general. The key question is: what did the testator intend?

Re Slater [1907] 1 Ch 665 is a good example of the difficulties where there has been a change in substance. Here, there was a gift of stock in Lambeth Waterworks. After the date of the will the stock was taken over by the Metropolitan Water Board and Metropolitan stock was given in lieu. The court decided that the gift could not take effect. Why? If the gift was specific, there was ademption. Although the distinction 'specific' or 'general' depends upon the words used, i.e., the expressed intention of the testator, ademption does not depend upon the testator's intention, but on the question as to whether the property bequeathed is part of the assets on death. '. . . You have to ask yourself where is the thing which is given?' said Cozens-Hardy MR in *Re Slater*. The court concluded, on the question of intention, that the gift was general. The gift could not take effect, however, for there was nothing of equivalent value which would enable the personal representatives to acquire property for the beneficiary.

The changes may be in form only, for example, from shares to stock, as in *Oakes* v *Oakes* (1852) 9 Hare 66, or a splitting of shares as in *Re Clifford* [1912] 1 Ch 29. Where Government securities are converted on amalgamation or re-construction, the enabling Act would need to be studied to see whether the change is formal or substantive. Where a re-construction of shares in a limited company is proposed, the company may offer additional shares and/or cash to encourage the shareholders to agree to the re-construction. Although ademption would be avoided if the original subject matter of the gift is traceable, any additional shares or a cash sum given will not carry with the original gift, see dicta in *Re Kuypers* [1925] Ch 244.

The will 'speaks from death'

In dispositions of property the will is construed as if it were executed immediately before the death (s. 24, Wills Act 1837), unless there is a contrary intention expressed in the will itself, or if the subject matter is described in such a particular fashion that the description can only mean the property held at the date of the will. Read the judgment in *Re Sikes* [1927] 1 Ch 364 where in a gift of 'my piano' the court concluded that the testatrix intended to give the piano owned at the date of the will and not a piano acquired after the will and owned at death.

In construction questions watch for the inclusion of a later codicil to the will. If the codicil confirms the will, then the will is regarded as being republished as at the date of the codicil in accordance with s. 34, Wills Act 1837. Republication will not save a gift which has been adeemed; see, for example, *Re Galway's Will Trusts* [1950] Ch 1. However, republication may alter the construction of a gift which would otherwise be adeemed. A good example is *Re Reeves* [1928] Ch 351 where the subject matter was a lease which, following expiry by effluxion of time, was renewed after the date of the confirmatory codicil. The gift was described as '. . . my present lease of . . .', that is, expressing a contrary intention, the subject matter of the gift answering the description at the republished date.

Ademption and the doctrine of conversion

Suppose by his will Dennis devised his freehold property 'The Gables' to Ron, the residuary realty to Kate and the residuary personalty to Alan. If, after the date of the will, Dennis enters into a contract for the sale of 'The Gables' to John, the effect is to adeem the devise to Ron and the proceeds of sale of the property would pass to Alan. The reason is that the contract of sale converts the realty to personalty. Suppose instead that Dennis had given John an option to purchase 'The Gables' exercisable within three months of Dennis's death. If John takes up the option the effect is the same, the devise to Ron is adeemed and Alan will be entitled to the proceeds of sale. Equity looks at the intention of the parties and treats the capital as being converted from the date of the grant of the option. This principle is expressed as the rule in *Lawes* v *Bennett* (1785) 1 Cox 167. Note the emphasis on capital. Where the property yields income this remains, from the date of the death of the testator, the entitlement of the specific devisee, Ron, until the exercise of the option.

Watch again for the effect of republication by a confirmatory codicil executed after the date of the grant of the option. Dennis is taken to be aware of the grant of the option at the date of the codicil, and is saying 'I still want Ron to take the property represented by the gift' (this would be the proceeds of sale following the exercise of the option, as in *Emuss* v *Smith* (1848) 2 De G & Sm 722). Similarly, in the case of ademption by contract, if the will is confirmed after the date of the contract, this is construed as an intention that the specific devisee should take the sale proceeds. *Re Sweeting (dec'd)* [1988] 1 All ER 1016 applied this principle to a conditional contract entered into after the date of the will. Once the condition was met, in this case the purchasers obtaining a satisfactory mortgage, then the transaction proceeded to completion.

The failure of gifts

Introduction

The importance of identifying the type of gift, the meaning and effect of abatement and ademption have been considered above. Ascertainment of the type of gift is also important in considering the consequences of failure of the gift. A specific or general legacy which does not take effect will fall into residue. If a residuary gift fails then, in the absence of a gift over in default, the property will be distributed according to the rules of intestacy.

A gift may fail to take effect for a number of reasons. By his will Oliver bequeaths to Henry 'my parrot, Arnold'. Henry may not want Arnold (oh dear), he may not wish to contract psittacosis (go on, look it up), or may not be prepared to insure such a valuable parrot. Henry may have pre-deceased Oliver or Henry's wife may have witnessed Oliver's will.

Disclaimer

A beneficiary cannot be forced to take the gift unless he has accepted it by conduct. Where the subject matter is a singular whole the beneficiary cannot disclaim part and accept the remainder. It is otherwise if there are two separate gifts.

Lapse

A cardinal principle of the law of succession is that the beneficiary must survive the testator in order to take the benefit. However 'lapse' is not confined to non-survivorship. A gift may lapse, for example, by the operation of s. 15, Wills Act 1837 and the meaning of lapse in relation to divorce or annulment of marriage has been considered in chapter 5.

Watch out for the effect of lapse where property has been given to two or more persons. If the property is to be held by them as joint tenants, then lapse of one share will mean that the property passes to the survivor under the *jus accrescendi*. If, however, the gift is to persons to hold as tenants in common then, where lapse occurs, e.g., because one party pre-deceases the testator, then that share will fall into residue. If the property consists of residue then, in the absence of a gift over, the lapsed share will devolve on intestacy as property undisposed by the will.

Can one avoid lapse? This is a matter of drafting. A general declaration against lapse will not suffice; however, a clear gift over in the event of failure is commonly used. An alternative is to express the benefit in the form of a class gift (see chapter 9 on construction). There are statutory provisions to save a gift from lapse, and in this book s. 184, Law of Property Act 1925 and s. 33, Wills Act 1837 are considered.

Section 33, Wills Act 1837

This is an important statutory exception to the doctrine of lapse. The section, though still cited as s. 33, was re-drafted by s. 19, Administration of Justice Act 1982. The new section applies to deaths on or after 1 January 1983.

When does the section apply? If ever there was a good example of the need to read examination questions carefully, this is it! The section applies where the testator makes a gift to his child or remoter issue and the beneficiary pre-deceases the testator, leaving issue who survive the testator. Not, note, a gift to a nephew who pre-deceases, or the testator's brother who pre-deceases, but to a child. The section has the effect of saving the gift to the child and, in the absence of evidence of a contrary intention (which must appear in the will) the surviving issue will take the gift on a per stirpial basis.

The complexities which surrounded the original s. 33 provided favourite material for examination questions. Despite the removal of some difficulties in the revised section, this statutory exception to lapse remains an important topic both in practice and in the examination room. A good illustration of the difficulties surrounding the operation of the original section is *Re Basioli* [1953] Ch 367.

Practitioners still prefer to include an express substitutional gift in the will rather than rely upon the statutory exception, for there is greater certainty and clarity in basing distribution upon an express provision where the testator's child pre-deceases. The revised s. 33(2) introduces the concept of statutory saving of the gift to class gifts (see chapter 9 on construction).

Commorientes

The word refers to the situation where persons die at the same time where it cannot be ascertained by clear evidence which person died first. Roman law provided a solution by raising a presumption on biological grounds that the grown up son was presumed to have survived the father. At common law the courts refused to raise any presumption as to the order of deaths. '. . . the English law has hitherto waived the question and perhaps prudently abandoned as devisive all those ingenious and refined distinctions which have been raised on this vexed subject by the civilians', said Chancellor Kent in his Commentaries. Therefore, in the absence of any presumption, where a beneficiary and the testator died in the same accident, or there was no clear proof as to survivorship by the beneficiary, the gift lapsed; see the dicta in *Underwood* v *Wing* (1855) 4 De GM & G 633.

The statutory presumption of survivorship of the younger in s. 184, Law of Property Act 1925 applies the presumption where it is 'uncertain' which person died first. The leading case on the construction of s. 184 is *Hickman* v *Peacey* [1945] AC 304. The Court of Appeal held that there could be no uncertainty where the parties died simultaneously (in this case a bomb destroyed a London house in 1940 killing all the occupants). By a 3:2 majority the House of Lords held that even the slightest doubt as to the order of deaths is sufficient to raise the presumption. Bear in mind that if there is clear evidence as to survival, by however brief a period, this evidence will prevail, for s. 184 is merely a presumption to save the gift from lapse. An alternative approach in the common accident situation is to base survivorship upon evidence on the balance of probabilities, as in the Scottish case of *Lamb* v *Lord Advocate* (1976) SLT 151. This approach is considered by some commentators as preferable to the statutory presumption, assuming that there is some evidence which could indicate a likely order of deaths.

Practitioners prefer the inclusion of a survivorship clause in the will making the benefit contingent upon survival for one calendar month, or a specified 28 days. This period is usually long enough to deal with a common accident situation but it is not too long so as to hold up the administration of the estate. A survivorship clause should not be included automatically in a will. Care needs to be taken to work out the ramifications for the distribution of the estate and a survivorship clause may not be desirable in dealing with liability to taxation. Further, where an express clause is included, care should be taken with the wording. The view of the majority in the Court of Appeal in the construction of the word 'coincide' in the will of the good Dr Rowland undid the doctor's intentions; see *Re Rowland* [1963] Ch 1. A return will be made to Dr Rowland and his wife in chapter 9 on construction.

A frequent addition to a question on commorientes is to have the elder spouse, as an alternative, die intestate. The aim is to note the non-application of s. 184 where the elder spouse, or both spouses, die intestate. Think through the effect of the statutory presumption to see the reason for this exclusion. Where the elder spouse dies intestate all that intestate's property would, on an application of s. 184, pass to the estate of the younger spouse and thereafter on the terms of the younger spouse's will or intestacy to the possible detriment of the blood relations of the elder spouse.

Forfeiture

One feature of expectancy of benefit under a will is that the beneficiary has to wait until the testator dies in order to take the benefit! The law takes a poor view of those who seek an early receipt of their benefit by accelerating the demise of the testator.

The common law developed a series of principles based upon public policy whereby benefit was denied not only to the perpetrator of the crime, but to those who sought to claim through the criminal. A good example is the civil action relating to the claims upon the Crippen estate following the execution of the infamous Dr Crippen for the murder of his wife, whereby relatives of the deceased wife prevented Crippen's mistress from inheriting any property belonging to Mrs Crippen; see the judgment in *the Estate of Crippen* [1911] P 108. The leading common law cases should be studied, in particular *Re Giles* [1971] 3 All ER 1141, where the public policy bar applied to a conviction of manslaughter on the grounds of diminished responsibility, thereby denying benefit to a surviving spouse on the resulting intestacy.

The Forfeiture Act 1982 gives the court a discretionary power to grant relief except in cases where the person is convicted of murder. The Court of Appeal in *Re K (dec'd)* [1985] 2 All ER 833 affirmed the decision of Vinelott J at [1985] 1 All ER 403 in granting relief under the Act. The judgment of Vinelott J should be read. In the judgment Vinelott J referred to the decision in *Re Giles* as having a bearing on the passing of the Act. In *Re Giles* Pennycuick VC refused to consider the question of moral culpability in the killing. Vinelott J pointed out that the purpose of the 1982 Act '. . . as I see it is to entitle and indeed require the court to form a view on that very matter'. Section 2(2) refers the court to the question of conduct of the offender and of the deceased, and to such other circumstances as appear to the court to be material. Other circumstances would include the relative financial position of a person claiming relief and the others with claims under the testator's will or intestacy. This raises an interesting issue, namely, the relationship between judicial discretion under the Forfeiture Act 1982 and discretionary powers to order financial provision for an applicant under the 1975 Inheritance (Provision for Family and Dependants) Act. The statutory rules on forfeiture do not preclude a killer from applying for provision under the Inheritance Act 1975 unless he has been convicted of murder (ss. 3 and 5 Forfeiture Act 1982). However, an application for provision from the estate would not succeed where the deceased's will or intestacy would have made reasonable provision for the applicant if the forfeiture rule had not applied, see the judgment in *Re Royse* [1984] 3 All ER 339. Look for points in problem questions where the facts point to possible culpability on the part of a beneficiary, thereby inviting you to apply the statutory provisions as interpreted by the judgments in *Re K*.

You are unlikely to face in an examination the dilemma of the beneficiary in New York where the wealth testator left substantial property to his parrot for life, with remainder over to the beneficiary charged with looking after the parrot. Parrots are known for their longevity and our New York bird, in its cage overlooking Central Park, was overheard to call 'infamy, infamy, he's always got it in for me' every time the remainderman approached the cage! A short course in aerobics is now suggested before turning to the next chapter, chapter 9, on construction.

Problem

The following is an illustration of a problem on s. 184, LPA 1925 and a suggested framework answer.

Harry and his wife Wilma died last week in a car crash. By his will Harry left his freehold property, Blackacre, to his nephew, Dan and the residue of his estate to Wilma; but if she pre-deceased him, then to his niece, Emily. Wilma by her will left all her estate to Harry; but if he pre-deceased her, then to her nephew, George. Shortly before his death Harry had entered into a contract for the sale of Blackacre but completion has not yet taken place. Harry and Wilma do not have any other close relatives.

Consider the entitlement to their respective estates:

(a)   where the evidence shows that Harry survived Wilma by a few hours;
(b)   where there is no evidence to show the order in which the deaths occurred;
(c)   where there is no evidence as to the order of deaths and Harry or Wilma died intestate.

At common law there is no presumption as to survivorship where there is no evidence as to the order of deaths; *Underwood* v *Wing* (1855). However s. 184, Law of Property Act 1925 says that where two or more persons die in circumstances rendering it uncertain which of them survived, the other such deaths are presumed to have occurred in order of seniority. Can one say that there is uncertainty here where a car crash has happened, perhaps causing instantaneous death? 'Yes', says the House of Lords in *Hickman* v *Peacey* (1945) per Lord Macmillan, where the slightest degree of uncertainty is sufficient to invoke the statutory presumption. If there is any evidence, on the balance of probabilities, then the evidence as to order should be applied; *Lamb* v *Lord Advocate* (1976). Here, with no evidence, Harry would be presumed to have died first. His residuary estate would pass to Wilma and thence, with the exception of Blackacre, to George. The gift of Blackacre would be adeemed by the contract as in (a).

If Harry, the elder spouse, had died intestate, the statutory presumption in s. 184 would not apply. Both spouses would be treated as having died at the same time; s. 46(3), Administration of Estates Act 1925. Therefore as Wilma has not survived, the residuary estate would pass to Emily and

Wilma's entire estate would pass to George. The reason for the non-application of the section is to avoid all the property going to one side of the family (in this case Wilma's family) to the exclusion of the family of the other spouse.

If Wilma had died intestate, then the statutory presumption would apply. The devise of Blackacre in Harry's will would be adeemed by the sale. The residue would pass to Wilma and go on her intestacy to her nephew, George.

NINE

CONSTRUCTION

Introduction

I am now going to outline two different reactions from students who turn to this part of the succession course. First, there is Ivor, who, somewhat daunted by the apparent volume of material, wonders where to begin. Secondly, there is Mort who, on the other hand, is the type who plunges straight into a problem without thinking through the facts, saying 'easy lah . . . read the will'. In their way both Ivor and Mort are right. The topic appears daunting in view of the number of cases and in trying to discover a clear pathway. In another way it is simply a matter of reading the will. Questions tend to be confined to the principal areas rather than the numerous secondary rules. Essay questions are popular, in particular quotes from the judgments of Lords Atkin and Simon in *Perrin* v *Morgan* [1943] AC 399. In addition, s. 21, Administration of Justice Act 1982 which deals with the admission of extrinsic evidence to clarify the meaning of words and phrases in the will must be carefully studied.

The dicta in *Perrin* v *Morgan* and subsequent cases, coupled with the provisions of ss. 20 (rectification) and 21 (extrinsic evidence) of the 1982 Act appear to indicate a shift in approach which would make the following words of Lord Atkin in *Perrin* v *Morgan* ring true:

> I anticipate with satisfaction that henceforth the group of ghosts of dissatisfied testators who, according to a late Chancery Judge, wait on the other bank of the Styx to receive the judicial personages who have misconstrued their wills, may be considerably diminished.

'See, what did I tell you?' says Mort, 'easy lah'.

The approach

The approach to the construction of a will can be summarised as follows:

(1)   Read the will, is it clearly expressed?

(2)   Place the will in context at the date of death. Who has survived the testator? What is the nature and the extent of the property at death?

(3)   If the meaning is unclear after reading, giving the words their ordinary meaning, look at the circumstances surrounding the testator when he made the will. This is applying the so-called 'armchair rule', see the dictum of James LJ in *Boyes* v *Cook* (1880) 14 ChD 53.

(4)   If there is equivocation, is there any extrinsic evidence which may be available and admissible? Useful articles to study on this difficult topic are by Dr C H Sherrin (1976) 40 Convey 66 and Leslie Blohm, 'Wills and the rules of evidence' (1983) NLJ, 23 December.

Historically the ecclesiastical courts borrowed heavily from Roman Law and many Roman Law principles were applied to the construction of wills of personalty. Today, in practice, it can be difficult to separate the functions of probate (Family Division) from construction (Chancery Division), since the Family Division has to construe a document as a will or look at more than one document to determine what, if anything, is admissible, for example in the 'envelope cases', or cases of possible implied revocation.

Begin at the beginning — a question of intention

The function of the court is to interpret the words used by the testator and not to make the will itself. The court looks at the will as a whole and not simply at the part in issue. In this way, other provisions may make it easier to determine the intention of the testator. The testator may, for example, give a definition clause in a later part of the will.

The words of the will are given their ordinary, grammatical meaning. The leading case was decided by the House of Lords; *Perrin* v *Morgan*. Here, the court had to construe the meaning of the word 'money'. This is not easy for one cannot simply turn to a dictionary. The word has changed its meaning over the years. Also the word can mean different things to people of differing backgrounds. See, for example, the dictum of Goulding J in *Re Barnes's Will Trusts* [1972] 2 All ER 639:

No doubt the use of a word like 'money' varies between persons of different classes, possibly between different parts of the country, certainly in the mouth of one and the same individual under differing circumstances, and a judge would need to be more of a philologist than I am to feel confident in relying in all cases on his own knowledge of the contemporary use of the English language. Nevertheless, it seems to me that the House of Lords has directed that a judge should apply his own knowledge of the language in the light of such context and circumstances as may assist him.

The courts approach the meaning of a will with caution. To go back to basics, the will represents the last wishes of the testator, the will must be in writing. What do these written words mean? The approach is not: what did the testator intend? Do the words carry out that intention? If not, then change the words. One can only approach the meaning by construing the actual words used.

The following words of Lord Simon in *Perrin* v *Morgan* are frequently quoted and form a popular examination question:

> My Lords, the fundamental rule in construing the language of a will is to put on the words used the meaning which, having regard to the terms of the will, the testator intended. The question is not, of course, what the testator meant to do when he made his will, but what the written words he uses mean in the particular case, what are the 'expressed intentions' of the testator?

In studying the approach the judgments in *Perrin* v *Morgan* should be read. Do not however lose sight of the kind of word the court was asked to consider, the word 'money' with its shifting meaning.

Contrast the words of Lord Simon with the dissenting judgment of Lord Denning in the Court of Appeal in *Re Rowland (dec'd)* [1963] 1 Ch 1. Brief reference was made in chapter 8 to Dr Rowland. The case is a good illustration of the pull between the strict constructionalist approach of the ordinary meaning of a word, and the intentions of the testator. Consider what Dr Rowland and his wife had in mind when they set about making their wills using (they had not met Lord St. Leonards!) will forms. Why did they think of their wills? They were to depart for the South Seas where the doctor would ply his skills among the Polynesian Islands. They had no children. They wanted to leave their property to one another but, if one pre-deceased or their deaths should coincide, then the doctor left his property to his relatives and, in a similar will, his wife left her property to her relatives. They perished when a ship on which they were travelling from island to island was lost in circumstances where there was no evidence as to who died first. Wreckage was found days later but no bodies, and the likeliest explanation was that the unfortunate people would have provided a meal for the sharks!

The question before the court was whether to apply the statutory presumption as to the order of deaths in s. 184, Law of Property Act 1925, or whether the will provided for a common accident? The approach divided two ways: (1) what was the ordinary grammatical meaning of the word coincide? (2) what did Dr Rowland mean by the use of the word 'coincide', i.e., what did he intend? The majority of the Court of Appeal went for approach (1); the word coincide meant no more and no less than dying at the same time. Since this added nothing to assist in establishing who died first, then the statutory presumption should apply. Lord Denning in a strong dissenting judgment, adopted the alternative approach asking, in his Hampshire burr:

> What did the good Doctor mean? He meant 'if we should die together then my property is to go to my family and your property is to go to your family'.

Lord Denning could cite the words of Lord Simon in *Perrin* v *Morgan* when he said:

> I now turn to some of the reported cases, premising only that it seems to me a little unfortunate that so many of such cases should find their way into the books, for in most instances, the duty of a judge who is called on to interpret a will containing ordinary English words is not to regard previous decisions as constituting a sort of legal dictionary to be consulted and remorselessly applied whatever the testator may have intended, but to construe the particular document so as to arrive at the testator's real meaning according to its actual language and circumstances.

Lord Denning applauded the approach of the House of Lords in *Perrin* v *Morgan*. However, in the light of his dissenting judgment he was criticised for encouraging possible uncertainty in the construction of wills. The danger is to ascribe too 'loose' a meaning to a word which has a definite meaning in an attempt to arrive at a view of the testator's intention. In defence Lord Denning cited the words of Lord Simon (see above): . . . 'the fundamental rule . . . is to put on the words used the meaning which, having regard to the terms of the will, the testator intended', and agreed that one must have regard to the meaning of the words, but (and this is the crux) the meaning ascribed to them by the testator. The reply by Lord Denning is woven into the dénouement in 'The Merchant of Venice' and the defence speech by the disguised Portia defending the anguished Antonio, quoted in his Lordship's book, *The Discipline of the Law* (London: Butterworths, 1979).

The key to the approach by the House of Lords is in the remainder of the quote from Lord Simon, supra, i.e., 'what are the expressed intentions of the testator; that is, what do the words which the testator has used mean?

In eliciting the avowed intention of the testator the court resorts to the 'rules of construction', that is, rules of convenience used to assist them in a task which the seventeenth century Chief Justice Coke recognised as difficult when he said, '. . . wills and the construction of them do more perplex a man than any other learning'; *Roberts* v *Roberts* (1613) 2 Bulstr 123.

The principal rules of construction

Usual meaning

Words are given their ordinary, grammatical meaning. Recourse will be had to the *Oxford English Dictionary*. Where a word has changed in meaning, such as the word 'money', then the meaning is that attributed to the word at the date of the will; *Perrin* v *Morgan*.

The word will be considered not only in the context of the phrasing of a particular clause but according to the tenor of the will as a whole. Suppose, after a series of specific legacies and devises the testator leaves' . . . the remainder of my effects . . .'; in the context of the will as a whole this could be interpreted as a general residuary gift.

The ordinary meaning of the word will not be applied if, in considering the intentions of the testator (which intentions are gleaned from reading the will as a whole) it would lead to absurdity.

Secondary meaning

The wording of the will itself could indicate a secondary meaning to the word. *Re Davidson* [1949] Ch 670, a case on the construction of technical words, is a good illustration. Here, a residuary gift to 'my grandchildren' was held to include the children of the testator's step-son because in the will the step-son was described as 'my son' and one of his children as 'my grand-daughter'.

In order to give the will greater dimension the document must be read not only in relation to the situation at the death of the testator (i.e., who survives the testator? What property does he own at death?), but in the light of the circumstances at the time the will was made. The reading by reference to the circumstances at the date of the will can indicate a secondary meaning. A good illustration is *Re Smalley* [1929] 2 Ch 112 where the testator gave all his property to 'my wife Eliza Ann Smalley'. His lawful wife, Mary Ann, survived him. However, he lived with a woman called Eliza Ann Mercer who believed herself to be his lawful wife. Reading the will in the context at the time of execution it became clear that the testator used the word 'wife' in a secondary sense, meaning his common law wife. Another good illustration is the shortest litigious will. In *Thorn* v *Dickens* [1906] WN 54 the testator simply wrote 'all to mother'. These were very clear words, except extrinsic evidence showed that by the time of the execution of the will the testator's mother had died! What did he mean? The surrounding circumstances showed that he was in the habit of referring to his wife as 'mother'.

The evidence may not show clearly that the testator intended a secondary meaning. The court will then apply the ordinary grammatical meaning where this provides a certain meaning, even though the result may appear capricious. Study the facts in *Gilmour* v *MacPhillamy* [1930] AC 712 where the ordinary grammatical meaning of the word 'survivors' was applied which gave the will a certain meaning, although it is likely that the construction placed on the words by the court did not reflect the intention of the testator.

Technical words and phrases

The approach of the judiciary, in seeking to apply certainty and avoid generalities in expression, is to presume that the testator intended the technical meaning to prevail unless the context of the will itself (as in *Re Davidson*), or the circumstances applying at the date of execution (as in *Re Smalley*), indicate a meaning which rebuts the presumption. This approach spells danger for the well-intended but ignorant person, or the 'barrack-room' lawyer, that is, the lay person who strives conscientiously to make his own will but who 'to make it more legal' throws in some phraseology such as 'male issue' or 'heirs', not realising, as the ghost of Lord St. Leonards rises above him, that the courts will usually apply a strict interpretation to technical words or phrases. In *Re Cook* [1948] Ch 212 the testatrix used a printed will form to make her will leaving 'all my personal estate whatsoever' to her named nephew and nieces. The estate mainly consisted of realty. The court construed the words as meaning personalty as there was nothing in the will to suggest a secondary meaning. The result was that the bulk of the estate passed on intestacy as being undisposed by the will.

Words omitted or changed

A clause in the will is construed by reading the will as a whole. In order to give a clear meaning to the clause the court may conclude, by looking at the will as a whole, that words have been omitted. How does this square with the courts' admitted reluctance to write a will for the testator? The function of the court of construction is to give effect to the intentions of the testator by placing a certain meaning on the words used. If it becomes clear that in order to give effect to the perceived intention, it is necessary to read the will in a particular way so as to arrive at the perceived intention, then the court will do so. In *Re Whitrick* [1957] 1 WLR 884 the testatrix left her entire estate to her husband and provided that 'in the event of my husband . . . and myself both dying at the same time' her estate should be held on trust for X, Y and Z equally. The testatrix's husband pre-deceased her. If the words of the will were read literally then the gift to X, Y and Z failed. The whole tone of the will, however, was to the effect that if her husband did not survive the testatrix, X, Y and Z were to take. Therefore, to give effect to the perceived intentions, the will was read to give effect to the gift to X, Y and Z in the event of the husband pre-deceasing.

Where the court is faced with irreconcilable provisions in the same instrument, reading the will as whole may indicate which provision should prevail. If there is no clear indication, then the courts have opted for the last condition as applying for this is (literally) the last will of the testator. This is clearly a rule of last resort used to uphold a gift.

Care should be taken in studying the approach here. The power to supply, omit or change words is very limited and must spring from the intention apparent in the meaning of the words used. This is a matter of construction and is not the same as the statutory power of rectification in s. 20, Administration Act 1982 referred to in chapter 3.

Codicils

Refer again to chapter 5 on revocation of wills. A codicil to a will is construed as secondary to the will. Therefore where a will or codicil contains a gift expressed in clear terms, a reference to the gift in a later codicil is not construed as revoking the earlier gift unless there is a clear intention to revoke. A good example is *Re Wray* [1951] Ch 425, noted in chapter 5.

The admission of extrinsic evidence

An important question in the construction of wills is how far can one admit evidence outside of the will to arrive at the expressed intentions of the testator. This is not an easy question to answer and the texts cite a multitude of cases together with the propositions laid down by Sir James Wigram VC, the 'Wigram Rules'. These rules and early cases on construction should be read selectively in view of the application of the statutory rules for the admission of extrinsic evidence in s. 21, Administration of Justice Act 1982 which apply to the construction of the wills of testators dying on or after 1 January 1983. The provisions of s. 21 amount to a codification of the rules concerning extrinsic evidence. In order to appreciate the statutory provisions the approach of the court and the nature of extrinsic evidence need to be studied.

The court of construction cannot look at the original will to correct any error for the probate copy of the will is considered to be conclusive. However, the court can refer to the original will to see how the will was set out, for example, if punctuation marks were used. Where, however, the will contains total blanks extrinsic evidence cannot be used to construe what should be there.

Keep in mind the four points of the summary of the approach set out at the beginning of this chapter. The will must be placed in the context at death. It is at this stage that questions of possible lapse, ademption or abatement arise. One moves to a further stage in the process to consider the admission of evidence to determine intention.

Two key distinctions must be drawn. One is between direct and circumstantial extrinsic evidence. The other is the distinction between the latent and the patent ambiguity. '£1,000 to one of my brothers' is patently ambiguous; '£1,000 to my brother' when the context shows that the testator has two surviving brothers reveals a latent ambiguity.

Direct extrinsic evidence would include instructions for the will and any statements made by the testator as to his intention. Suppose by his will Tom leaves '£1,000 to my friend, Johnny'. At death the will is placed in context and reveals that the testator had two friends called John — John Jeeves and John Wooster. The fact that Tom told a friend that he intended to give £1,000 to Johnny Jeeves is direct extrinsic evidence. The fact that Tom knew John Jeeves and habitually referred to him as 'Johnny' is circumstantial extrinsic evidence.

In cases of deaths prior to 1 January 1983 the admission of extrinsic evidence is governed by the case law. Direct extrinsic evidence as to intention was inadmissible unless there was equivocation, that is, where the description of an object or subject is to apply to two or more persons or things. A good example is *Re Jackson* [1933] Ch 237 where the testatrix left property to 'my nephew, Arthur Murphy'. At death the context revealed that the testatrix had three nephews called Arthur Murphy, two legitimate and one illegitimate. As a side point consider what would have happened if there had only been two nephews, one legitimate, the other illegitimate (see the references to legitimacy in chapter 6). The law at that time, applying the principle in *Hill* v *Crook*, would have only recognised the legitimate nephew; therefore there would have been no equivocation. However, the fact that there were two legitimate Arthur Murphys revealed equivocation in the form of the latent ambiguity — which nephew? Evidence admitted as to the intention of the testatrix showed that she intended to benefit the illegitimate nephew.

Circumstantial extrinsic evidence was admissible in the case of deaths pre-1983 as an aid to uncertainty or ambiguity. This evidence was admissible under the 'armchair rule'. A good example of the admission of extrinsic evidence arising from uncertainty is *Charter* v *Charter* (1874) LR 7 HL 364. Study the facts and see how the House of Lords allowed evidence of the surrounding circumstances which revealed which of the two surviving sons was closer to their father and the object of his bounty.

Where a person satisfies the description in the will, then circumstantial extrinsic evidence will not be admissible, save in exceptional circumstances, to alter the direction of the gift. In *NSPCC* v *SNSPCC* [1915] AC 207 the testator gave a legacy to the NSPCC. Evidence showed that he had lived all his life in Scotland and the testator had never shown an interest in the English charity. The House of Lords ruled that this evidence was not enough to rebut the presumption in favour of the NSPCC where the description in the gift matched exactly the name of the English charity. Perhaps this is a case where a mistake in writing the description of the gift could, at the end of the day, have achieved the testator's real intention for, if there had been uncertainty, the evidence of his Scottish connections would have indicated the intended direction of the gift. This case is a good example where the court will not interfere where the words used convey a clear meaning.

Deaths after 1982

The provisions of s. 21, Administration of Justice Act 1982 must be carefully studied. The section allows the admission of both direct and circumstantial extrinsic evidence in three situations.

First, where any part of the will is meaningless. This would not appear to assist where there is a blank for there is nothing on which to fasten a meaning. However, where e.g., the testator has used a code, then circumstancial extrinsic evidence could be admitted to interpret the code. In *Kell* v *Charmer* (1836) 23 Beav 195 extrinsic evidence was admitted under the 'armchair rule' where the testator had used a jewellers' code to give sums of money.

Secondly, in the case of an ambiguity on the face of the will, the patent ambiguity. To allow direct evidence as to intention represents a change in the law. Previously only circumstantial extrinsic evidence was admissible, for example, in a gift of 'my money' or 'my effects', circumstantial evidence would be admissible under the armchair principle. Study the dictum of Nicholls J in *Re Williams* [1985] 1 All ER 964 where a letter from the testatrix to her solicitor was ruled to be admissible in order to clarify the division of the groups of beneficiaries in the will, albeit the letter did not in the end prove to be of assistance. In *Re Tepper's Will Trusts* [1987] 1 All ER 970 the court had to consider whether gifts conditional upon remaining within, and marrying within 'the Jewish faith' were void for uncertainty. Scott J took the view that the provisos appeared to be void for uncertainty. However, although direct evidence of the testator's intention was inadmissible, extrinsic evidence could be adduced as to the testator's practice of the Jewish faith so as to attribute a sufficiently certain meaning to the term.

Thirdly, where the gift is ambiguous in the light of the surrounding circumstances, that is, the latent ambiguity such as the equivocation revealed in *Re Jackson* (1933). Suppose Tom by his will leaves '£500 to my nephew, James Arthur Green'. At death he is survived by two nephews, one called James Green, the other, Arthur Green. Extrinsic evidence would be admissible to assist in the interpretation of the language used. However, to end at the beginning, in admitting extrinsic evidence the court will not re-write the will for the testator. As Nicholls J stated in *Re Williams* '. . . if . . . the meaning is one which the word or phrase cannot bear, I do not see how, in carrying out a process of construction . . . the court can declare that meaning to be the meaning of the word or phrase'.

Reprise

Ivor has contained the volume of material by considering in broad terms the approach to construction, distinguishing the types of evidence and examples of ambiguities and picked out a selection of cases. He has then studied carefully s. 21 and the comments upon the section by Nicholls J in *Re Williams (dec'd)* and Scott J in *Re Tepper's WT* and planned a framework of an essay on construction. Mort on the other hand contemplates the mirror prior to going on the town and says 'I told you, easy lah!'.

Section 24, Wills Act 1837

Section 24 is authority for the proposition that in construing the will the will 'speaks from death'.

A will does not become effective until the death of the testator. In construing the descriptions of property the will is read as if it were executed immediately before the death of the testator unless there is a contrary intention appearing in the will itself. The effect, therefore, of s. 24 is to enable a will to deal with after acquired property so, for example, 'all my freeholds' would mean all freeholds owned at the death of the testator unless there is a contrary intention denoting, for example, a description at the date of the will. A good example of a contrary intention is *Re Sikes* (see chapter 8). In considering the operation of s. 24, watch for the effect of republication by a later codicil which confirms the will. This has the effect of altering the description amounting to a contrary intention to the date of the codicil as in *Re Reeves* (see chapter 8). Section 24 does not apply to the description of persons; here, the person entitled is the one answering the description at the date of the will, see *Re Whorwood* (1887) 34 Ch D 446.

Questions on construction

Essay questions often take the form of a quote from *Perrin* v *Morgan* and invite an explanation of the judicial approach to the construction of wills.

The following are examples of the kind of problems which can form a question on construction of the will. The name of the testator is Tom.

'My 400 shares in Gokart Limited to my nephew, Paul'. At the date of the will Tom owned 600 shares in Gokart Limited which he retained until his death.

'My estate in Scotland to my son, Alan, but if he dies before me, or at the same time as me, then to my brother, Ben instead'. The day before Tom's death, Alan went mountain climbing alone, he was never seen alive again and was found dead two days later.

'My Surrey house "The Gables" to my nephew, David'. One month before his death Tom had exchanged contracts for the sale of 'The Gables' for £180,000 but he died before the completion of the sale. The purchaser obtained a mortgage a week after Tom died and the sale was completed four weeks after the death of Tom.

Tom leaves the 'remainder of my money' to his daughters, Harriet and Jean in equal shares. Harriet died two months before Tom, survived by her son, Bob.

Class gifts

Note the definition of the class gift given by Lord Selbourne in *Pearkes* v *Moseley* (1880) 5 App Cas 714. Suppose Tim by his will leaves the residue of his estate to his nephew, Sam and his niece, Violet for life and after their deaths on trust for such of their child or children who attain 21 in equal shares. The residuary gift is a class gift, for the persons who could share are uncertain in number at the time of the limitation but answer to a general description so that they can be identified. The class gift is indeterminate until such time as all those are identified who ultimately answer the description, here, in Tim's will, being the children born to Sam and Violet. In order to ensure property passes without delay the courts have devised a series of rules to apply closure to the class at the earliest opportunity. In advising upon the determination of the class closure two key dates must be identified, the date of death of the testator and the date of distribution. In an immediate class gift these dates will be the same. If Albert left his residuary estate to 'my nephews' the class would consist of all those nephews alive at the date of Albert's death.

Consider carefully the rules on class closure. The gift in the will of Tim is an example of a postponed class gift. The date of distribution will be the death of the survivor of Sam and Violet. If a child is alive at the death of Tim but dies before the last life tenant, the estate of the child will still benefit provided the child attained 21, for the child has survived the testator and met the contingency in the gift, see for example, *Re Sutcliffe* [1942] Ch 453.

Note the situation where the life tenant surrenders his life interest. Suppose in the case of Tim's estate, that Sam and Violet decide to release their life interests thereby accelerating the remainders. Does this decision cause a premature closure of the class which would normally stay open until the deaths of Sam and Violet? In *Re Davis* [1957] 1 WLR 922 Vaisey J held that a surrender did effect an early closure of the class. However, Stamp J in

Re Kebty-Fletcher's Will Trusts [1967] 3 All ER 1076 disagreed and doubted the correctness of *Re Davies*. The decision of Stamp J was followed by Goff J in *Re Harker's Will Trusts* [1969] 3 All ER 1. The constructional rule relating to class closure, known as the rule in *Andrews* v *Partington*, which says that the class must close at the earliest opportunity was only to apply to reconcile inconsistencies in the will. In these cases on surrender there was no inconsistency therefore the class was to remain open until the death of the life tenant.

The revised s. 33, Wills Act 1837 (see chapter 8) applies to class gifts (s. 33(2)). Suppose John by his will dated 1 October 1978 leaves his residuary estate 'to my children in equal shares'. John had two children, Alice and Ben. Ben died in 1986 leaving two children, Lucy and Mike who survive. John died in 1992. Under the original s. 33 the class would consist of Alice. Hence, to allow for benefiting issue an express provision was preferred whereby a per stirpial distribution could take place to Ben's children. Under the new section the express provision of a per stirpial clause is no longer necessary because the section allows Ben's issue to benefit. The residue would be divided as to half to Alice and a quarter each to Lucy and Mike.

TEN

THE ADMINISTRATION OF THE ESTATE
PART ONE — IN THE BEGINNING

Introduction

This is a vast area of study. Topics include types of grant and the obtaining of the grant to the estate; the powers, duties and liability of the personal representatives; the administration of the solvent and the insolvent estate and the transmission from administration to trusteeship. Whatever the nature of the course of study you are pursuing under the heading 'Succession', care needs to be taken to see where the emphasis lies in this area of probate practice. The purpose of chapters 10 and 11 is to comment upon certain areas as an aid to study. The approach to this part of a succession course should be to read carefully the particular syllabus and see where the emphasis is laid, and note the areas which require an outline knowledge only and then turn to the text, support materials and authorities.

Types of grant

Return to basics. The will, although an important document before death (so do not place a coffee cup on it or more particularly do not staple anything to it!) does not become effective until the death. However, the will alone does not provide the authority to distribute the assets of the deceased. The will must be submitted to the court. Approval by the court is signified by the issue of the grant of representation to the estate.

There are three key types of grant to keep in mind in the administration of the estate. Probate, which issues to the executor who proves the will; administration with will annexed, where there is a valid will but no proving executor and administration on intestacy, where there is no valid will. Reference is made to other types of grant, for example, *de bonis non administratis* or *caetorurum* (the grant issued to general executives where a limited grant has already been issued), but grants such as these, issued for particular purposes, are an adjunct or a part of the three main types.

Personal representatives

Executors

Executorship is a personal office which cannot be assigned. The executor is usually appointed by the will of the deceased and the 'person' is the testator's choice charged with administering the estate at death. The authority of the executor stems from the will. Appointment of executors can be express or implied. In express appointments there may be constructional problems if, for example, the appointment is ambiguous; resort may then be had to extrinsic evidence which is considered in chapter 9. Note the difficulties which may occur where a firm (as is often the case for firms of solicitors) is appointed as executor. This is construed as an appointment of all the members of the firm as at the date of the will, subject to the proviso in s. 114(1), Supreme Court Act 1981 which limits the number to four initially in respect of the same estate. Power would be reserved for the remaining partners to prove if one or more appointees dropped out. To overcome possible difficulties in the appointment of a firm (for example, the firm could have merged, been taken over, split from the date of the will to the death of the testator, see the suggested clause which received judicial approval in *Re Horgan* [1971] P 50. Where professional people are appointed as executors it is usual to include a charging clause in the will to enable profit costs charges to be made. A charging clause is treated as a legacy (!) therefore a professional appointee or that person's spouse should not witness the will!

Consider how the implied appointment of the executor can arise. Watch the situation where a person is named in the will coupled with a direction to pay just debts, this may not amount to an implied appointment. Contrast the situation of implied appointment of a person 'according to the tenor of the will' as *In the Goods of Cook* [1902] P 115, with the intention to make a legacy subject to the payment of debts as in *Re Fawcett* [1941] P 85.

Although a person may be named as executor in the will, the court has the power by virtue of s. 116, Supreme Court Act 1981 to pass over an executor, for example, where the executor is insolvent or, as illustrated in the case of *Estate of S* [1967] 2 All ER 150, where the person named was serving a prison sentence at the time of the death of the testator. The overriding consideration is to ensure that the appointment is in the best interests of the estate as a whole. Look for the short examination question in this area: 'The executor is not necessarily the person named by the testator' — discuss. This involves a study of s. 116 (together with consideration of the 'chain of representation') and the inherent power vested in the court of passing over persons of known bad character. Contrast for example where the person named is in known financial difficulties. This in itself is not a bar, however, if that person subsequently becomes insolvent the court will appoint another.

A person cannot act as an executor where he or she is under the age of eighteen or is of unsound mind. Contrast the situation where another person is named along with the person who is under age or otherwise incapable and the situation where the person who lacks capacity is named as the sole executor. The latter situation is an example where a grant of letters of administration with will annexed would be made, limited in time to the person of incapacity. Note also that s. 50, Administration of Justice Act 1985 allows personal representatives (that is, the executor or administrator) to retire from their duties if they so wish and gives the court power to appoint substitutes.

Continuity of office

An advantage in appointing an executor rather than relying upon administration is the statutory power of continuity of office in s. 7, Administration of Estates Act 1925, the so-called 'chain of representation'. Section 7 will apply where a person named as executor accepts the office and obtains the grant but dies before completing the administration of the estate. If the deceased executor has appointed an executor to his own estate who is able and willing to prove, that executor becomes executor by representation to the original estate. The purpose of the section is to provide continuity therefore reducing possible delay in the administration of the estate. Study the situations where the chain would be broken, for example, where the succeeding executor fails to prove the will of the deceased executor, or where the original appointment was to the estate as a whole, whereas the succeeding executor's appointment is limited to a part of the estate, such as a business or copyrights.

Note the following situation which could arise in practice. The deceased (T) by his will names two people A and B to act as his executors. A proves the will with power reserved to B. A then dies before completing the administration of the estate and appoints F to be his executor. F wants to administer A's estate but what should he do when he becomes aware of B? If F simply proceeds with the administration of the estate of A, he (F) automatically becomes executor by representation to the estate of T. B could then come along and prove in T's estate. F should issue citation to make B decide whether he wishes to prove in the estate of T, see the judgment in *the Goods of Frengley*.

A problem with the chain, as seen in the example above, is that the succeeding executor, F in the example, cannot choose simply to administer A's estate and not act in the estate of T. A possible solution is if the succeeding executor would be entitled to a grant of administration in the estate of the deceased executor. Suppose A is the sole executor to T in the above example. F could break the chain by renouncing the appointment as executor to the estate of A and then apply to administer A's estate by applying for a grant of letters of administration with will annexed. This would be possible provided F was entitled to apply for administration and the court accepted this course of action. The criterion the court would adopt would be the best interests of the estate as a whole.

Commentators see the chain in s. 7 as a rather dated concept. Perhaps a more preferable way to provide continuity would be to give personal representatives similar powers to those enjoyed by trustees, namely, the last surviving trustee or the personal representative of the last surviving trustee has the power to appoint new trustees, thereby ensuring continuity.

A person named as executor faced with a possible chain of estates needs to be aware that one does not have to accept office formally. Doing any act commensurate with the office of executor, for example, collecting assets and paying some debts constituted acceptance in *Re Stevens* [1898] 1 Ch 162. Contrast this with the reluctance to act where a formal renunciation of the appointment must be filed with the court. Once a renunciation is filed, it cannot be retracted without the consent of the court; see rule 37, Non Contentious Probate Rules 1987. Again, the criterion adopted by the court in deciding whether to allow retraction is the best interests of the estate as a whole. Renunciation on the basis of incorrect legal advice, as a sole reason, is not considered to be a valid reason for a retraction; see *the Goods of Gill* (1873) 3 P & D 113.

Administrators

Where there is no executor able to prove the will of the deceased, or the deceased has died intestate a grant of administration will be made. Entitlement to a grant of administration is determined either according to an interest under the will in accordance with rule 20, NCPR 1987, or the entitlement on intestacy under rule 22. The rules as to capacity to be an administrator are similar to executorship. Note that where there is a minority or a limited interest under the will or intestacy at least two administrators must be appointed, whereas in the case of executorship the court has a discretion whether to appoint additional executors.

The *executor de son tort*

The term '*executor de son tort*' refers to a person who, without lawful authority, assumes the role of lawful personal representative and carries out acts which only a lawful executor or administrator could do. Case authorities are few on this topic but note the principles which have emerged. Contrast an act which could constitute a person executor de son tort, such as continuing the business of the deceased without authority, with an act of necessity or charity such as caring for the stock of a deceased neighbouring smallholder. An intermeddler is liable to the lawful personal representatives to the extent of the assets received, but the wrongdoer can plead in defence that the assets have been applied in a lawful manner. Liability can ensue however innocently a party may have acted, as illustrated by the judgment in *New York Breweries Co. Ltd* v *Attorney General* [1899] AC 62, a case which acts as a warning to company secretaries. Interesting litigation, which included an application to constitute personal representatives executors de son tort, occurred in connection with the liability to pay death duties following the death of the leading industrialist Sir Charles Clore in *IRC* v *Stype Investments (Jersey) Ltd* [1982] Ch 456, where the Court of Appeal held the personal representatives liable as executors de son tort in diverting sale proceeds from an English freehold out of the jurisdiction to Jersey. Although Stype had been named as personal representatives, their action in diverting the moneys to accounts in Jersey was ruled to be intermeddling in the proper administration of the English estate. The related action to this whereby the Official Solicitor was appointed to deal with the outstanding tax liability is cited as *Re Clore (dec'd)* [1982] 2 WLR 314.

The offices of executor and administrator contrasted

The property of the deceased devolves upon the personal representative in his capacity as personal representative. Therefore should the personal representative subsequently be adjudged personally bankrupt the trustee in bankruptcy cannot touch the estate assets.

The executor takes his authority from the will and can therefore do any act prior to the issue of the grant which does not require the production of the grant, for example, the executor could pay debts and exchange contracts for the sale of land although he could not complete title to the land without production of the grant of probate. The administrator on the other hand takes his authority from the order of the court. Until the grant of letters of administration is issued the property of the deceased vests in the court and the administrator is entitled to do only those acts which are necessary in order to obtain the grant. This would entail, for example, compiling the inventory of assets and liabilities in order to complete the Inland Revenue account, filing the account together with the payment, where applicable, of death duties together with the original will if the application is for administration with will annexed. A person entitled to administration has no authority to do any additional act in relation to the administration of the estate before the letters of administration are issued. So, for example, a settlement of a claim by an administrator prior to the issue of the grant is not binding on the estate, see *Mills* v *Anderson* [1984] 2 All ER 538. Further, the administrator has no power to commence litigation prior to the issue of the grant. A good example of the practical application and unhappy consequences of this rule can be seen by reading the judgment in *Ingall* v *Moran* [1944] 1 All ER 97.

An executor on the other hand can commence proceedings before the issue of the grant of probate. An interesting case on the power of executors was the action taken by the executors to the estate of the late Peter Sellers concerning the use, without permission, of film clips and discarded film material from earlier films in producing a new film out of the material. Cited as *Rickless* v *United Artists Corporation* [1987] 1 All ER 679, the Court of Appeal ruled that the right to give the consent for reproduction of a performance was not personal to the actor but vested in his personal representatives.

Revocation of grants

The court has the power under s. 12(1) of the Supreme Court Act 1981 to call in a grant which should not have been made or one that contains an error. Note the kind of circumstances where the court would order a revocation of the grant. An obvious situation is where administration has proceeded on the basis that the deceased has died intestate and, sometime later, a will is found which is considered valid and admitted to probate. Less obvious is the situation which arose in *the Estate of Napier* (1809) 1 Phill 83 where a grant was obtained and the testator was found to be alive!

A grant can be revoked where the personal representative leaves the jurisdiction in circumstances where it is unlikely that he will return; as in *the Goods of Loveday* [1900] P 154 where the widow obtained a grant following intestacy, but disappeared before completing the administration of the estate. The disappearance in Loveday constituted 'special circumstances' resulting in the revocation of the grant to the widow. Compare the decision in *the Estate of Cope* [1954] 1 All ER 698 where lack of full disclosure of assets was not a reason for revocation, the correct course was to apply for an order to supply an inventory under s. 25, Administration of Estates Act 1925. On the other hand proof of dishonesty would give rise to revocation where it is believed that the beneficiaries would be seriously prejudiced. Mental or physical disability on the part of the personal representative can give rise to revocation.

Note the effect of s. 27, Administration of Estates Act 1925 which protects third parties who have dealt in good faith with a personal representative whose grant is revoked. Tactically, in a situation where, e.g., the administration of the estate has slowed because the personal representative keeps going abroad, the beneficiaries or some other person entitled under either rule 20 or rule 22 should cite the personal representative to show cause why he is not proceeding with the administration and, if the response is unsatisfactory, apply for revocation of the grant.

The duties of the personal representative

Broadly, the duties are to obtain the grant to the estate as expeditiously as possible, gather in the assets of the deceased, assess and settle the claims upon the estate and distribute the remainder of the assets according to the terms of the will, intestacy or a combination of both. Until the grant is obtained bank accounts remain frozen and investments cannot be transferred, so it is imperative that the grant is obtained as quickly as possible.

Challenges to the will

Where the personal representative is applying in respect of a will, either as named executor or administrator under rule 20, NCPR 1987, the original will and any codicils must be filed with the court. It is at this stage that a challenge to the validity of the will would be made, for example, for want of valid execution in accordance with s. 9, Wills Act 1837, or in respect of the ability of the testator to form the necessary *animus testandi*. The judge may raise a query where, for example, the wording of the will does not appear to be rational, or the court is not satisfied as to the validity of the attestation. The will may be damaged in some way or contain pinholes. The judge can call for further evidence by affidavit. The principal affidavits to be aware of are due execution, usually sworn by the witnesses, assuming that they can be traced (this is the reason that the witnesses are asked to print their names and addresses on the will); plight and condition, pinholes in particular can cause a problem, where, e.g., the testator has stapled the solicitor's letter enclosing the original will to the will itself and this has, with the passage of time, become detached. To the court the hole could indicate another testamentary document. The affidavit of plight and condition is usually sworn by someone in whose safe keeping the will was placed. The affidavit of search would be used where the will or a codicil is undated or the dates do not match, sworn by someone instrumental in the preparation of the document.

The challenge may come from someone alleging want of execution or capacity. Refer to chapters 2 and 3 particularly on burdens of proof. How would a challenge start? A person who believes that there is a case to challenge the will, or the entitlement of the purported personal representative to obtain the grant, would lodge a caveat or warning with the court. This effectively puts a stop against the estate. The caveator can be cited to show cause why the caveat should not be removed. If the caveator adduces evidence supporting the challenge, then probate would proceed in solemn form, that is, following the pattern of civil litigation with the writ, statement of claim, defence and the pleadings of either side.

Alternatively the personal representatives themselves may apply to the court for a summons for directions, asking the court to pronounce upon the validity or otherwise of a disposition, for example, in *Re Jones* (1981) (chapter 4) which concerned the validity of an oral statement made by a dying soldier in Northern Ireland.

The applicant for the grant must prove entitlement to act. The person may be named as executor in the will. If the application is by an administrator, the oath sworn by the administrator will refer to entitlement to apply either under rule 20 or rule 22. It may be that there is a person entitled to administer who is higher in the order under rule 20 or rule 22 but that that person is doing nothing about the administration. It is open for a person lower in the order to issue citation to clear those with a prior entitlement in order that the administration may proceed without delay.

Study what is meant by 'assets' in s. 32(1) Administration of Estates Act 1925 and the property which is not available for the payment of funeral, testamentary, administration expenses, debts and death duties. This is important in relation to the studies of the administration of the solvent estate, see chapter 11. Debts should be paid promptly and careful attention given to the assets which may have to be sold in order to pay the debts.

Different types of grant

There are numerous 'special grants' relating to the administration of an estate. Study the reasons for the main special grants, in particular the grant *de bonis non administratis, ad colligenda bona* and *pendente lite*. (Mort thinks that these are the half back line of an Italian football club but Ivor knows better.) *De bonis non administratis* means literally 'of the goods not yet administered'. An example of where this grant would apply is where there has been a break in the chain of representation. *Ad colligenda bona* is issued where assets are in need of urgent attention, for example, where estate assets at death include 'perishables'. One might describe this as the 'tomato grant'. Where the personal representatives in the Clore estate (see above) showed a lack of urgency in dealing with the death duty liability, the Official Solicitor successfully applied for a grant *ad colligenda bona* to expedite the settlement of tax due from the estate.

The grant *pendente lite* is not a brand of lager but applies where a probate action has commenced, e.g., a challenge to the validity of the will, and it is necessary to safeguard estate assets during the currency of the action; see s. 117, Supreme Court Act 1981. Usually the grant will issue to a neutral party unless the parties to the action consent to someone acting who has an interest in the action. The appointee has all the powers of a general administrator, except that the appointee is not permitted to distribute estate assets to the beneficiaries without the leave of the court. Contrast this form of grant with the situation where there is no personal representative of the deceased and it is necessary for the estate to be represented in legal proceedings, for example, where the estate is being sued in negligence arising from a motor accident. In this case a grant of administration limited to the action (*ad litem*) may issue under s. 116, Supreme Court Act 1981.

These points are merely a 'flavour' of the differing special grants. Study in particular the reason for the different types of grant rather than simply learning a list.

The liability of personal representatives

On application for a grant both the executor and the administrator have to swear oaths that they will duly administer the estate according to law. Beneficiaries who suspect maladministration can sue the personal representative on the oath. The will may contain a clause relieving the personal representatives in cases of wrongdoing. The usual form of clause used to this effect restricts liability to wilful and individual fraud or wrongdoing on the part of the person to be made liable and relieves him from liability for mistakes made in good faith or for the acts or defaults of co-representatives or agents. The effect of such a clause is to restrict liability so far as the beneficiaries are concerned. Alternatively, if there is no such clause, the beneficiaries may agree among themselves that a personal representative may be relieved of liability. This agreement is effective so long as all the beneficiaries are *sui juris*. A clause or an agreement can protect the personal representatives against the beneficiaries, but the right of creditors to proceed against the personal representatives remains unaffected.

Note the statutory protection given under ss. 23 and 27 of the Trustee Act 1925. Under s. 23 a personal representative is not liable for loss to the estate caused by an agent appointed by the personal representative, provided that the agent was appointed in good faith. Section 27 protects the personal representatives from claims by creditors of whom they are unaware, by requiring the personal representatives to advertise for debts and claims against the estate.

The statutory advertisements will not protect personal representatives if they are aware of the rights of a particular beneficiary but cannot find the beneficiary at the death of the testator. The personal representatives must advertise for claims and, in order to expedite administration, they can apply to the court for a 'Benjamin Order' permitting distribution of the estate on the basis that the beneficiary who cannot be found has pre-deceased the testator, and so his entitlement has lapsed; see *Re Benjamin* [1902] 1 Ch 723. The court can impose such conditions as it thinks fit, for example, ordering distribution of the assets subject to a contingency fund to meet a possible claim; see *Re Gess* [1942] Ch 37.

Section 61 of the Trustee Act 1925 enables the court to grant relief to a personal representative or a trustee where the person has acted in good faith, reasonably and ought fairly to be excused. This power, which can apply against creditors as well as beneficiaries, is discretionary. The court is not under a duty to grant relief and will consider each case upon its merits.

Actions against the estate in contract and tort in general survive the deceased. There are exceptions, for example, contracts involving personal services and defamation actions in tort. A point to watch is where a business forms part of the assets at death and it is necessary to continue the business operations in order to protect the value of the goodwill. Care should be taken in advising personal representatives in this situation, for they can be personally liable to creditors for post-death debts even though they contract in their capacity as personal representatives.

Devastavit

The liability of the personal representatives for acts in the course of administration of the estate is collectively known as *'devastavit'*, meaning literally 'he was wasted'. There are three main headings under the umbrella of *devastavit; viz.* (1) misappropriation of assets, (2) maladministration and (3) a failure to safeguard assets. Misappropriation would include, for example, using estate assets for personal use or entering into collusive sales. Suppose one of the assets is a near new motor car with a low mileage. If the personal representative uses the vehicle extensively thereby increasing the milage and reducing the sales appeal, the personal representative could be liable. Maladministration would include paying debts in the wrong order where the estate proves to be insolvent (a personal representative could only plead no knowledge of the debt if he had placed the correct advertisements as required by s. 27, Trustee Act 1925); failing to dispose quickly of a wasting asset such as an uneconomic lease thereby incurring additional expense upon the estate; failing to pay a debt promptly so that the creditor sues the estate or a delay in obtaining probate leading to a loss of investment opportunities. Failure to safeguard assets refers to negligence by a personal representative. The standard of care is low, equivalent to that of the gratuitous bailee, so the personal representative would not be responsible for the loss of estate assets in the absence of proof of wilful default.

Example of a problem

The following are examples of the type of problem in relation to the entitlement and liability of personal representatives, and serve to pull together some of the strands in this wide area of study.

(a)   Clem, a widower, died five months ago. By his will made in 1988 he appointed his former partner, Morgan, to be his sole executor and left his entire estate to his daughter, Gemma, who survives him. In the first four weeks following the death of Clem, Morgan arranged the funeral, collected insurance monies on Clem's life and paid the funeral account. Since then Morgan, who spends long periods looking after his business interests in New York, has done nothing with the estate.

Last week the Inland Revenue wrote to Gemma asking for the reason for the delay in dealing with possible liability to taxation. The estate is valuable and includes extensive farmlands, and two paintings believed to be by Turner. Gemma turns for advice to her uncle, Dan, Clem's estranged brother, an actor with a local repertory company. Dan informs Gemma that he will 'sort matters out' and takes two rare vases from the farmhouse and sells them to Noddler, an auctioneer friend. Dan keeps the sale proceeds 'to defray expenses' and pays the electricity and telephone accounts relating to the farm out of the sale of grain stocks.

Advise Gemma.

(b)   Tom died recently having appointed Simon and Paul to be his executors. Shortly after the death of Tom, Paul died intestate and, three months later, Simon died. By his will Simon appointed Alice and her younger sister, Beth to be his executors. Alice says she wants nothing to do with Tom's estate.

Advise Alice and Beth.

ELEVEN

THE ADMINISTRATION OF THE ESTATE
PART TWO — PROCEEDING TO THE END, BUT WHAT
COMPLEXITIES LIE AHEAD?

In this chapter the administration of the insolvent estate is considered. This is an important area in practice but not a popular question in degree papers because the approach is simply a matter of categorising the types of debt. The administration of the solvent estate which follows is another story. This is a favourite area for the examiner in view of the complexities and the absence of a House of Lords' authority. Finally consideration is given to the end of the administration period and the transition from administration to trusteeship.

The insolvent estate

When the testator dies, the personal representatives should collect in and value the assets and assess liabilities. If it is clear that the value of the assets is going to be insufficient to meet all the liabilities, then the estate must be administered in bankruptcy. Debts must be paid in accordance with the statutory order laid down by s. 228, Insolvency Act 1985 and the Administration of Insolvent Estates of Deceased Persons Order, SI 1999/ 1986. Priority is given to funeral, testamentary and administration expenses and thereafter the order of debts in bankruptcy. Even where there is a possible doubt in the minds of the personal representatives as to whether the value of the assets will be sufficient to meet liabilities, the estate must be administered as if it were insolvent for, if the personal representatives do not take this course of action and the estate subsequently proves to be insolvent, they will be liable for *devastavit*.

Problems involving insolvent estates usually make it quite clear in giving the value of the assets and liabilities that the estate is insolvent. Then it is a matter of placing the assets stated in the problem in the correct category. Problems usually concentrate upon a selection of preferred debts, examples of deferred debts and the options open to the secured creditor. The insolvent estate is a relatively straightforward area of study. This cannot be said of the next topic, a favourite in degree course examinations.

The solvent estate

Introduction

Ivor, after careful study, is satisfied that he has a grasp of the main issues in the approach which the court adopts to the construction of wills. Mort on the other hand has become lost in a haze of direct and circumstantial evidence, but recovered somewhat in considering the role of the personal representative, the executor de son tort and the different grants — despite the initial confusion in thinking *de bonis non, ad colligenda* and *ad litem* all played for AC Milan. Mort, however, now looks utterly perplexed as he sees the look of concern that crosses Ivor's face as he turns to consider the statutory order for the application of assets in ss. 34 and 35 of the Administration of Estates Act 1925.

This topic relates to the incidence or burden of debts. The debts must be paid in full and from the point of view of the individual creditor he need look no further than the personal representatives for payment. The personal representatives then have to consider, as between the beneficiaries, which assets are to be used in the payment of debts. In other words, where does the burden of the debts fall? The question is clearly important from a practical viewpoint for one beneficiary is, perhaps, going to bear a greater burden of the debt than another. The issue is also a popular one for academic study for there is no House of Lords' decision on the interpretation of s. 34(3). The topic is known as the marshalling of the assets because the assets have to be 'marshalled' or placed into categories for the payment of debts.

The golden rule is to read the will to see if the testator has given any indication which assets should be free from the burden of the debts, and which must bear the burden. The question, 'does the wording of the will alter the statutory order for the application of assets?' is not an easy one to answer.

Debts charged upon property

Where debts are charged on property, for example, a mortgage debt secured on realty, s. 35, Administration of Estates Act 1925 makes the property primarily liable for the payment of the debt. The section applies to the extent that the debt is charged on the property, so in *Re Birmingham* [1959] Ch 523 where the testatrix had entered into a binding contract of purchase before her death, the specific devisee of the property was entitled to the property, subject to the vendor's lien for unpaid purchase moneys, but he did not have to bear the legal costs incidental to the transaction. The burden of these costs fell upon the residuary estate.

One has to consider whether the debt is charged on the asset. Suppose that the testator leaves an unincorporated business to X. The 'business' is an entity consisting of goodwill, stock and other assets on the one hand and debts on the other. The debts are not by their nature charged on the assets of the business unless there is a clear expression that this is the case, so the legatee takes the business free from the debts.

Where separate properties are charged with separate debts and the debt on one property exceeds the value of that property, the deficit is made up from the general estate and not from the other charged properties. This applies even where the charged properties are all given to one beneficiary; see *Re Holt* (1916) 85 LJ Ch 779. If, on the other hand, the properties are given as one composite gift, the deficit is made up from the other charged properties, see *Re Baron Kensington* [1902] 1 Ch 203.

The testator can negate the effect of s. 35 by a written direction, either in the will or by deed; for example, 'I devise "The Lodge" to Ken free of all debts'. A simple direction that debts are to be paid from the residue would be insufficient to exclude s. 35. However, the contrary intention need not be express but can be made by implication. Study, as an example, the judgment in *Re Valpy* [1906] 1 Ch 531 where the debts, excluding a particular mortgage debt, were charged on property. The specific exclusion of the mortgage debt was construed as an implied intention to throw this debt on to the residuary estate.

The incidence of general debts — the marshalling of the assets

This process consists of classifying the real and personal property of the deceased into a series of notional funds so that no fund in the marshalled series is exhausted. The statutory rules are intended to give effect to what may be presumed to have been the wishes of the testator. The testator can indicate in the will which assets are to bear the burdens of the debts, that is, varying the statutory order. The problem is what form the direction should take, for there is a paradox in the statutory order. To understand the problem the statutory order for the application of assets in s. 34(3) and Part II of the First Schedule to the Administration of Estates Act 1925 must be studied and thoroughly known. The consideration of the problems in this chapter pre-supposes a knowledge of the order.

The statutory order in s. 34(3) can be varied by a direction to the contrary in the will. The problem is in deciding what amounts to a direction sufficient to vary the statutory order. In the statutory order property undisposed of by the will is the primary fund for the payment of the debts. *Re Lamb* [1929] 1 Ch 723 ruled that a lapsed share of residue is property undisposed of by the will.

A typical problem question on this topic would be as follows:

By his will, Colin, who died this year, gave

(a)   £16,000 to Len;
(b)   All sums owed by Colin and secured by mortgages, to Michael, but subject to the payment thereout of all Colin's debts;
(c)   The residuary real and personal estate to trustees on trust to sell and to hold the proceeds in trust for Peg and Olive equally.

Peg died before Colin.
Colin's estate consists of £30,000 secured by mortgages, other personalty worth £20,000 and realty worth £50,000. The debts amount to £40,000.
How would the estate be distributed?

Issues which arise here are: (i) Does the statutory order apply? (ii) Is the direction in (b) sufficient to vary the statutory order to the extent of the £30,000? Peg's share lapses (there is no suggestion on the facts that, for example, s. 33 would apply to save the gift to Peg), therefore if the statutory order does apply, then her share is primarily liable for the payment of the debts. (iii) Where does the burden fall in respect of the pecuniary legacy to Len?
    At this stage Ivor starts to thumb through the list of cases. Mort sighs and decides that he has a thirst, for a drink rather than knowledge.

The problem

The statutory order can be varied by a direction to the contrary in the will. What amounts to a direction sufficient to vary the order? A mere direction to pay debts is insufficient, for the personal representatives are under a duty to pay the debts in any event.

Variation by definition of residue

Residue, as referred to in the studies on succession, means what is left after all the debts and liabilities have been met. So, where Steven by his will leaves the remainder of his property whatsoever and wheresoever to Chris and Jeannie in equal shares absolutely then, provided that the estate is solvent, Chris and Jeannie know that they will take whatever is left after all the debts, liabilities and other interests under the will have been settled. However, for the purposes of the marshalling of the assets 'residue' takes on a different meaning. 'Residue' is number two in the order whereby the assets are placed in categories before the debts have been paid. Therefore, if there is a lapsed share of residue, as in *Re Lamb* [1929], this would become number one in the order and primarily liable for the payment of the debts, leaving the surviving residuary beneficiaries in category two.

The order can be varied by wording the gift of the residue in such a way that the residuary share cannot be ascertained, and, therefore, cannot be divided in the event of a lapsed share, until the debts have been paid. In *Re Kempthorne* [1930] 1 Ch 268 the testator bequeathed 'all my leasehold property and all my personal estate and effects . . . subject to and after the payment of my funeral and testamentary expenses and debts and the legacies bequeathed by this my will . . .'. There was a lapsed share of residue. Was this primarily liable for the payment of the debts? 'Yes', said the court at first instance for the direction was merely to pay the debts. 'No', said the Court of Appeal, the wording was such that the residue of the estate could not be ascertained until the debts had been paid. The issue is important in practice where there is a lapsed share. If the lapsed share is primarily liable, then the surviving residuary beneficiaries will take a greater share of the assets. If, on the other hand, the order is varied in the manner of *Re Kempthorne*, then the whole of the remainder bears the debts before the division, therefore those entitled on the partial intestacy arising from the lapsed share will bear the burden of the debts equally with the residuary beneficiaries. Study the judgment in *Re Kempthorne* and note the form of words which effected the variation. In *Re Harland-Peck* [1941] Ch 182, again in the Court of Appeal, the words 'subject to the payment of . . .' which preceded the gift of residue were held to vary the order. Read the judgment of Luxmore LJ where he considers variation of the order. Again in *Re Berrey's Will Trusts* [1959] 1 WLR 30 the words 'after all my debts . . . have been paid' preceding a gift of residue varied the order.

Variation by bequest or charge

The testator could vary the statutory order by specifically bequeathing property or charging particular property with the payment of debts. Does this in itself vary the order? At first glance this would appear to be the case, until the statutory order itself is re-read, where property bequeathed for the payment of debts, and property charged with the payment of debts are not numbers one and two in the order but numbers three and four. A mere appropriation or charging will not vary the order, as illustrated by *Re Gordon* [1940] Ch 769. In this case there was no other expression of intention regarding the debts, see the judgment of Bennet J.

What does amount to a bequest or charge which varies the order? In *Re Meldrum* [1952] Ch 208 there were bequests together with a reference to the payment of legacies, funeral expenses and debts cast in such a way as to make a deposit account primarily liable for the payment of the debts coupled with an intention to exonerate the residue.

'. . . it seems to me to remain a question purely of construction of each will whether or not the testator has varied the order of application of assets or not' per Upjohn J in *Re Meldrum*. In *Re James* [1947] Ch 256 the testator gave specific property to his bank as executor on trust for sale 'after the payment of my just debts', the residue to his wife. The residue appeared to be the primary fund for the payment of debts, but Roxburgh J decided that by making the specific gift subject to the payment of debts immediately preceding the gift of residue, the testator intended to vary the order. The bank could not carry out the direction to invest moneys to create the residue without first paying the debts.

The incidence of legacies

The statutory order for the payment of debts does not specifically refer to the payment of legacies save in the case of the preservation of a fund to pay the pecuniary legacies. As a result the courts have been undecided as to whether the order applies to the payment of legacies: 'yes', says *Re Worthington* [1933] Ch 771; 'no', says *Re Thompson* [1936] Ch 676. The court in *Re Thompson* said that where the statutory order is unclear as to whether the provisions apply to legacies then one should apply the pre-1926 rules.

Pre-1926

Before 1926 general legacies were payable out of the personal estate which was not specifically bequeathed, subject to any contrary intention in the will. This had the effect of exempting real estate from the payment of general legacies, with the consequence that, where the personalty proved insufficient, one would not resort to the residuary realty unless the will showed an intention to resort to realty. What approach did the courts adopt? The courts have adopted two approaches in ruling that realty could be used to pay general legacies:

(a)   In *Greville* v *Brown* (1859) 7 HLC 689, where the testator by his will gave general legacies and the residue of his personal and real estate in one mass, the court ruled that the realty could be resorted to once the personalty had been exhausted. Property is given in one mass if there is no distinction between realty and personalty, for example, 'I give the remainder of my property whatsoever and wheresoever to A and B in equal shares absolutely'.

(b)   Where the testator, by his will, directed legacies to be paid out of a mixed fund of realty and personalty. In *Roberts* v *Walker* (1830) 1 R & My 752 the court held that the consequence of this approach was that legacies were payable rateably out of realty and personalty according to the respective values of the funds.

Rules post 1925

How far has the 1925 legislation altered the rules on the incidence of legacies? Section 33(2), Administration of Estates Act 1925 makes property undisposed of by will primarily liable for the payment of legacies whether the property consisted of personalty or realty. The issue in *Re Worthington* [1933] Ch 771 was whether the principle in *Greville* v *Brown* applied, making the personalty primarily liable (whether or not property passed on intestacy) or whether s. 33(2) altered the order. The Court of Appeal said that s. 33(2) applied. The following words of Lawrence LJ are popularly quoted to form an essay question on this tortuous subject:

> In *Re Kempthorne* the Court of Appeal . . . brought debts into line with legacies . . . I can see no real difference between debts and legacies and I think that legacies ought to be brought into line with debts.

There is uncertainty where the will imposes an express trust for sale and there is a lapsed share of the residue. The express trust excludes the trust implied by s. 33(1). Does s. 33(2) apply to the lapsed share? The position is unclear and the judgments in *Re McKee* [1931] 2 Ch 145 and *Re Beaumont's Will Trusts* [1950] Ch 462 need to be carefully studied.

The relationship legacies and the order in s. 34(3)

On a partial intestacy, for example, where there is a lapsed share of residue, the property undisposed of is primarily liable for the payment of the debts. Legacies are payable primarily out of the fund set aside in the order for the payment of legacies. Suppose that this fund is exhausted but legacies remain to be paid; s. 33(2), altering the pre-1926 rules, says that the balance of the legacies is payable out of the undisposed of share. Study the wording of s. 33(2): the order of resort is different from that laid down in paragraphs 1 and 2 of the order in s. 34(3). Under paragraphs 1 and 2 the pecuniary legacy fund is set aside first and the balance of the undisposed of fund (paragraph 1) or property comprising the residuary gift (paragraph 2) is liable for the debts; see *Re Anstead* [1943] Ch 161.

Has the statutory order in s. 34(3) altered the rules on the incidence of legacies? As indicated in the introduction to this headache (Mort returned but has gone out again) there are two views. One view is that the old rules, that is pre-1926, apply. This view is supported by *Re Thompson* (1936) and *Re Anstead* (1943). What is the effect? A fund for the payment of the legacies would only be retained from the lapsed share if the share would have been liable to bear the burden of the legacies under the old rules. This would also be so in the case of paragraph (2) and a retention of a fund from the residue. In both *Re Thompson* and *Re Anstead* the court held that the principle of construction in *Greville* v *Brown* applied. In *Re Beaumont's Will Trusts* (1950) Danckwerts J reiterated the view, *citing Re Thompson*, that s. 34(3) had made no provision as to the payment of legacies.

The alternative view is that s. 34(3) has altered the rules. The cases have all been concerned with the interpretation of paragraph (1) of the order. See *Re Midgley* [1955] Ch 576 where Harman J took the view that a fund must be retained from paragraph (1) to meet the pecuniary legacies irrespective of whether the undisposed of property would have been liable to meet the legacies under the old rules.

Time has passed and Mort has returned to hear the explanation of the issues by a now weary Ivor. 'Given such uncertainty' says Mort, 'why does this problem not appear more often in practice? After all, the consequences of the burden of debts and legacies can result in a greatly reduced benefit for one party as against others'.

Ivor, pleased that Mort appears to have grasped some of the problems, points out that in practice the draftsman will seek to ensure that the form of the residuary gift will be worded in such a way that the residue cannot be ascertained until the debts and legacies are paid.

The end of the administration period

There is no statutory definition of the end of the administration period. In practice the final distribution of the assets to the beneficiaries, and the handing over by the personal representatives of the signed estate accounts should mark the end of the period. Where the will disposes of absolute interests to the parties who are all *sui juris*, that is the end of the matter. However, the will may create limited interests, such as a life interest with remainders over, or contingent interests. In these situations, at the end of the administration period, a trust will arise. A personal representative can be sued after the end of the administration period for wrongful acts done during the period. For example, an infant beneficiary, on coming of age, can obtain a grant to the estate after the end of the administration period to call the personal representatives to account.

Frequently in wills the personal representatives are named as both executors and trustees. The personal representative winds up the estate and distributes the assets. A trustee holds the assets until a special event occurs, for example, the end of a life interest or a beneficiary meeting a contingency such as a specified age. Why is it important to distinguish between the two offices? In the case of the personal estate, the personal representatives have several authority, whereas the authority of the trustees is joint. This important distinction and its practical effect is well illustrated by studying the facts and the judgment of the House of Lords in *Attenborough* v

Solomon [1913] AC 76. In the case of real estate the authority of both is joint. However, it is important in practice that once the administration period has been concluded, the personal representatives formally assent to themselves as trustees. Consider the complications that can arise where there is no formal assent, as in *Re King's Will Trusts* [1964] 1 All ER 833.

Remedies of creditors and beneficiaries

Introduction

A number of points on the liability of personal representatives has been considered in these last two chapters dealing with the administration of the estate. The purpose of this final section is to pull together a number of these strands.

In the majority of cases the administration of the estate of the deceased proceeds smoothly from consideration of the terms of the will, or rules of intestacy, to the final distribution of assets to the beneficiaries. There may be instances, however, where the personal representatives need to seek the guidance of the court as to the validity or meaning of the will, or the beneficiaries wish to call the personal representatives to account. Resort will therefore be made to the court for assistance.

Administration by the court

Any person interested in the estate may issue proceedings for administration by the court. The applicant may be, *inter alia*, a personal representative, beneficiary or creditor. Application would be to the Chancery Division of the High Court under s. 61, Supreme Court Act 1981. There must be a duly constituted personal representative before the court would consider taking on the administration. The reason for this is that there must be a defendant to the proceedings. This person cannot be an executor de son tort because his duty is not to administer the estate, merely to account for what he has received. If no grant of administration has been made, creditors and beneficiaries interested in the estate may apply to the court for the appointment of a receiver to protect the estate pending the appointment of a personal representative. If there are proceedings pending in the estate a better course of action is to apply for the appointment of an administrator pending suit (*pendente lite*) under s. 117, Supreme Court Act 1981.

Administration by the court is expensive and the court will not make an order unless it considers it absolutely necessary. An example would be if the deceased had died bankrupt and it appears that it would be a complex estate for the personal representatives to administer, then, in the interests particularly of the creditors, the court would take on the administration. In many cases application to the court to take on administration will have been brought by the creditors or beneficiaries by way of calling the personal representatives to account, claiming that they have not acted properly. The court can, for example, order the personal representatives to account for legacies, debts or any property remaining outstanding. In addition the court can order the appointment of a person to act as a judicial trustee either alone or in conjunction with the personal representative.

The Limitation Act 1980 needs to be noted. In the case of creditors contemplating action against the estate, the limitation period is six years for a debt under a simple contract; the period runs from the date when the right accrued (s. 5). In the case of a judgment debt, the period is twelve years from the date when the judgment became enforceable (s. 24). These periods may be extended by acknowledgement of the debt by the personal representatives, either by part payment or in writing. The personal representatives themselves may apply to the court for specific relief, for example, on the meaning of a particular clause in the will, or on a summons for the court to pronounce on the validity of the will.

Actions against personal representatives

The nature and range of *devastavit* has been considered in chapter 10. A personal representative is personally liable if *devastavit* is proved. However, as has already been considered, certain defences can be pleaded, for example, s. 27, Trustee Act 1925 protection; the request to the court to exercise its discretion under s. 61, Trustee Act; an order to indemnify a personal representative under s. 62 where the beneficiaries or creditors have consented to the breach of duty; where a beneficiary or creditor in full possession of the facts and *sui juris* has acquiesced in the breach. A personal representative can plead *'plene administravit'* that is, not that he cannot eat any more pizza, but that he has duly administered the assets which have come into his hands. Under s. 48, Administration of Justice Act 1985 the personal representative can plead reliance on the opinion of a barrister as to the meaning or interpretation of the will. The barrister must be of at least ten years standing and give a written opinion. The opinion cannot be acted upon until the court so orders and the court will refuse where there are contentious issues which need to be aired before the court.

Action against the recipient of assets

Action against the personal representative will be the first course of action by the creditor or beneficiary. However, the personal representative may not have sufficient assets of his own to cover the value of the claim. The choices open in such a case are a personal claim against those who have received assets wrongly; as in *Ministry of Health* v *Simpson* [1951] AC 251, or to pursue a tracing action, see *Re Diplock* [1948] 2 All ER 318. However, these actions are more at home in the studies of equity and trusts than the world of succession.

'I've passed equity lah', shouts Mort in triumph.

INDEX

TITLE IN THE SERIES